Fifth Avenue Overhead

Bob Rosenthal

Edge Books

FIRST EDITION
Manufactured in the United States of America.

Cover art and design by Layla Sarakalo.

Photos used by permission are by Bob Rosenthal, Allen Ginsberg,
Bob Holman, Morris Rosenthal, Lewis Warsh,
and Steve Shames, at stephenshames.com.

Poetry sections by Richard Friedman, Peter Kostakis, Derek Steele,
and Ted Berrigan used by permission.

Edge Books are published by Rod Smith, editor of Aerial magazine,
and distributed by SmallPress Distribution, Berkeley, CA;
1-800-869-7553; www.spdbooks.org.

aerialedge@gmail.com   www.aerialedge.com

CONTENTS

CHAPTER 1

The Message   1

CHAPTER 2

Epistolary Year   9

CHAPTER 3

The Proposal   24

CHAPTER 4

Messenger   41

CHAPTER 5

Fifth Avenue Overhead   51

CHAPTER 6

A Place and a Time   72

CHAPTER 7

Heschel High   115

Fifth Avenue Overhead
is dedicated to my partner
for this past half century,
Rochelle Kraut.

1960 –1969

The Message

I am a body coming home to its head, ready for love. My solar birthday is in the dog days of summer, a good day for dying and being born. Everyone is somewhere else. My lunar birthday, the fourth of Elul, is an appointment everyone has to keep. The shofar blows; the time has come. Time to awaken the peacemakers in the family of who we are.

Shut up and take it. Tell the same story I always tell. A future without memory borrows music to dance the tunes of childhood's safe gauze. 1966, I am an avid reader of naturalism. I hold onto the grim lives of Studs Lonigan and Danny O'Neill. My own life is bumpy too. Father is a problem. He has a problem. He is adolescent and volatile. He hits. I have already given in to getting chubby. He makes me eat fast; I eat more to spite him. I stay within a fatted layer of protection. My fantasies are deep there. I keep them warm. I am an underachiever, undiagnosed learning disabled. My brother is smitten with ulcers in his colon; I am sent to a shrink prophylactically. Ulcers are thought to have a psychosomatic origin. This is all in the realm of my father's problem. He is a psychoanalyst who irrationally attacks his children for playing. He lacks ambition. He lacks philosophy. He remains a cipher. He only talks nicely if fed, with lit cigar, reading a psychoanalytic journal, while watching a football game on TV. Only now can Father be all ears. He offers indifference as his best interface.

Like a peony, I spring up early in my season and wait for the tiny feet of ants to unfurl my petals. Mother is a flower. She is a Rose in a valley of roses. She is my rock and redeemer. When I toss half-chewed food behind a radiator in the hall, she finds it as she vacuums. She looks up from the floor and stares at me, her face a conundrum. So I stuff it in my pockets to flush down the toilet to save her the work of deceiving Father. She never tells him. I learn to swallow without tasting. I go within the extra space I have. I am sad and lonely. I don't know what I want. But I do feel something will mitigate all the weekends alone in a big house. I know that I will enjoy my life; that I must be patient. In my attic room, I blow harp to Chicago blues, eyeing the orange glow to the South.

Strangely, I choose *Moby Dick* to read for its adventure. I soak up its wild nature and understand. We are all Ishmaels. Our lives become the changes we make along the way. Destinations are elusive. Distractions come front and center. The path reveals a map of Vietnam in the *Sun-Times* I cut out and pin to my wall, 1963. Mother assures me the war will be over before I am out of high school, 1968. The newsprint turns brown and crumbles from all its war years on that wall.

I read Father's old medical books. In Havelock Ellis I read about sexual practices. The cure for what I am doing is to insert a glass rod coated in silver nitrate up the urethra of the erect penis. Yes, that feeling works to help me abstain for a while. But I am in love with a girl down the block. She is in my morning carpool. She is cheery and loves to chat. Wanting love is confusing in my house. Mother once tells me she has to distance herself from being affectionate with me because Father fears I am becoming homosexual. For the one being ignored, a lack of attention is the best one can hope for. Reading *The Whale* is an act of self-reliance. I read a more current sex psychology book on Father's shelf and feel palpable relief that I will not be facing the glass pipette.

I imagine that I am the captain of a small stealthy boat. I command cadres of boats; they listen to me. I finally tell my psychiatrist my deep fantasy of battle prowess. This doctor doesn't pretend to pay attention. A plastic tub of candy in his closet calls out. I am free to get a piece anytime I want. I am pissed off. I buy an expensive candy bar in the lobby of the Carlson Building in downtown Evanston. Then I take the elevator to resist his candy. Slowly, I turn these dire sessions toward a target I don't have a map to. I realize I must stop wetting my bed. Hold. Hold. Hold it through the night. I put an end to therapy. Freshman year of high school, I am put in adaptive gym. Football jocks order us around while they lift weights. I do sit-ups and push-ups every night. I play the Chicago blues loud and build up my callisthenic counts. I test out of adaptive gym before the year ends.

I am myopic but don't realize it. I can't read the blackboard; I am drifting. Driver's education has a vision test, and I get glasses. The sudden inclusion of all the kids in the halls makes me gasp. I am a new driver buzzing the school when the Rolling Stones come on the radio "Satisfaction" — I can't get any! All of a sudden, I understand rock and roll. I start social service volunteering. I want to meet girls.

I lead a social service group to make friends. On Saturdays we bus to Chicago State Mental Hospital. The preadolescent ward is a single building on the large sprawling grounds. One end of the ward is the boys dormitory and the other end houses the girls dormitory. A large dayroom with a glassed-in nurses station separates the dormitories. The boys love to have us visit. They somewhat playfully beat up on us. No one gets hurt. They show us their stashes of Thorazine they pretend to take at night. The nurses overmedicate the kids for the nurse's own safety. The kids don't know what to do with all these pills.

There is a young social worker that visits the ward. He plays the out of tune upright piano in the dayroom. I get a strong message when he bangs out the new Rolling

Stones song, "Let's Spend the Night Together." The irony is not lost on anyone on the locked ward. The gospel chord progressions fill me with passions. I open the door to experiencing the emotions of love. I am still shy, but now I understand there is a destination to loving.

I love the Jewish girls in my social service group. One of them is dating an African American student. I am her shill. Her parents drop her off at my house, then the other guy picks her up. I am edging closer to love but not there yet. This is American gospel.

Wake up to Dionne Warwick's "I Say a Little Prayer". Go to school upbeat. I am driving Father's '64 Ford Falcon, three gears on the wheel and a manual choke. Seniors get parking privileges. Jane and Elizabeth are in the car every morning. The conversation makes me happy. It reminds me that I like life. Father is already starting to fade. I don't know what he is worried about. I got my special message. Just wait it out. I learn the art of indifference; get a job at Porters Pharmacy, saving up to buy my own car. High school ends without finding physical love. I am 18-years-old with a firm concept that I am real in the sense that one's own life can interest somebody else. I rule out thinking about my future my last year as a teenager.

*

Summer of '69, the revolution is still coming. It's grass, it's tabs of LSD, it's uppers and downers. Some kids are coming down; others are shooting up. The government is going to put a man on the moon. Everything is new to me as I come home to Wilmette, Illinois, with one year at the University of Iowa under my belt. Wilmette is an elderly suburb of Chicago that snuggles up to Lake Michigan and forms the southern end the North Shore community, noted for its extreme privilege. The house sits on Linden Avenue, only one and half blocks from the Chicago Transit Authority's terminus and within sight of the Baha'i House of Worship's dome. There are oak trees in the parkway before a crescent sidewalk that circumvents a low, wide juniper tree. The front door is behind a large dark screened-in porch. Inside live my parents.

I come in and turn up the volume – Bob Dylan's *Blonde on Blonde* runs up and down the stairs. I occupy my old room, which is a converted attic with slanted ceilings, drooping wallpaper, and a dark green carpet. My psychoanalyst father once used the room as a home-office to see patients. In the movie *Cobweb*, Richard Widmark, a shrink who runs a mental hospital, is married to Lauren Bacall. Their son is asked what he wants to be when he grows up; he answers, "A patient." When Father hears Dylan's vocal poetry, he asks me, "Who does he think he is kidding?" I don't aspire to be a patient. My attic room offers me enough privacy and space to hatch me in my *real* life.

I buy a used car using earnings saved from my drugstore job. Now I am driving a red VW Squareback with sunroof. I lean up against it to get my picture taken. I have my old summer job back, teaching developmentally handicapped children at the Shore School in Evanston. There are moments when life enlarges with new love; the warm summer evenings swirl around the white dome of the Baha'i House of Worship. I hardly see my parents, but when I do I find that I have outgrown the need to fight with them. I dream on my feet, open to everything.

Time is syncopated; there is an odd beat that hits me squarely in the face. I want soft Slicker lips and eyes to explore what's going on in there. I stand before a mountain of stored up desire. I want an avalanche of lips. I have crossed the frontiers of childhood to get here. I know this is my summer of fun. I'm ready. This boy has never been kissed.

I walk our old family dog, Maggie, around the block. In no time at all she pulls me up to my secret love just a few houses away. Jane is still a wonder of a buzzing girl nearly nutty being 16 years old. I rekindle the live embers of my carpool torch for her, tease her by calling her Little Bitty. Maggie and I bump into her on our very first walk of the summer. I am walking Maggie three times an evening. Maggie loves it. When I meet Little Bitty again, I arrange to give her a spin in my new car. We make a date to hear the Mothers of Invention on the lawn at Ravinia Park.

T minus five seconds – the Apollo rocket trembles on TV – the sound is off, the stereo plays Dylan:

You raise up your head	liquid oxygen releases
And you ask, "Is this where it is?	the garret falls away
And somebody points to you	the rocket is enveloped
and says "It's his"	by billows of vapor
And you say, "What's mine?"	three seconds
And somebody else says,	two seconds
"Where what is?"	trembling
And you say,	ignition
"Oh my God	flames
Am I here all alone?"	and blast off

Little Bitty is ready just yards away. I am too excited to eat. Now that chatter still works. We spread a red blanket on the lawn. Lie back and listen. Frank Zappa's intricate sieve of sound bounces off the trees to the leaves of grass. Little Bitty is not large but our first kiss is like stepping out into a new universe. Everyone on the lawn is kissing. I lean into lips and tongue that kiss back. Suddenly I realize that not a moment in my life is a waste! On the way home, we stop by the Northwestern Railroad tracks. I tell Jane that these are my first kisses so we kiss some more and the thrill makes me cry a little bit. We go to the Northwestern University summer film series and see *La Grande Illusione*. Erich von Stroheim asks, "Is it worth it? For a Rosenthal?" Yes. Little Bitty dates me several times; she has other boyfriends. I sometimes meet them while strolling with Maggie.

Working is a terrific part of my jellyroll adolescence. I work at the Shore School for special education summer camp for several years and am trained in behavior modification. I am working with a wacky woman from Rogers Park, with red hair, plump breasts, and a full deck of dirty jokes. Her sorority sisters call her Boobie-Doobie because her name is Donna Dubin. She is engaged to a man in Fort Wayne, Indiana, so we have a flirty ball in the classroom before she moves to Fort Wayne and catches pneumonia.

Here goes nothing. I ask a teacher named Pam out. I should know better because of my theory of names, which holds that I don't like Pams. Pam says, "Sure." It soon gets weird; all of a sudden Pam starts talking up her "boyfriend for years" to Donna. Donna tells me that Pam is up to something. Pam and I head back to Ravinia Park to hear B.B. King. No magic this time. Everything is stiff and cold and I am embarrassed as Pam questions me on how a boy from the suburbs turns out like me. But how am I? Not a jock. Not a nerd. Not a geek. We park on Sheridan Road at Morse Avenue; I make an awkward attempt to kiss her. I mumble some mumbo jumbo and somehow we do kiss. It is all wrong, wrong. I don't like Pam's kisses. My world is all kisses; they are either right or wrong. Pam says, "Should I make it easy for you?" What would you say? I say, "No." We kiss some more and say good night. I promise to call again; don't.

Donna has an extra ticket to a concert and no boyfriend around, so she asks me. Appropriately, I lock myself out of my car when I pick her up. I have to climb in through the open sunroof, which is not lost on the neighbors. Nor is it lost that Donna is going out with a guy who is not her fiancé. We have fun talking about it; after the concert, we each hold the end of a rolled-up program and skip around the parking lot. The only kissing is sweet goodnight kissing, which is utterly educational. Later in the year, at her wedding, she tickles my palm ever so lightly when we cordially kiss.

The last Tuesday in July is the payoff day. Here is an avalanche that lasts a lifetime. Donna is away; I am setting up art project with the kids. My volunteer, Cindy, is not following my instructions. I am getting peeved with her, when the director ushers in a new girl, skinny with short blonde hair and wide lapels on her dress. "This is Rochelle Kraut, Cliff Kraut's sister; she is here to observe you." I think, "Oh, shit!" I already have low regard for her brother; I once observed him almost clobber somebody with his befuddled attempts to fix a door. "This is bad," I think; worse yet is to have an observer when this stupid volunteer is giving me a hard time. I ignore Miss Kraut; camp goes on.

To my surprise, Rochelle is back the next day. Now she is our new volunteer. A blues lyric pops into my head. *I love the women. I love them all the same way.* But I don't pay her any attention at first. Later, she pricks up my ears when I say that I am going to the nurse's office to have a smoke (a cigarillo). Rochelle flirts with bright dancing pupils, "Oh, what are you going to smoke?" "Ha ha, later."

I am preoccupied getting ready to go to the first Ann Arbor Blues Festival. Little Bitty stands me up to watch the moon landing on TV. Dejectedly, I walk to the big pier in Wilmette Harbor and sit at the end facing my old friend, the moon. *Moon* is the first word I learn to say. The moon seems larger and closer, shining a yellow light over the boats in the harbor and the Baha'i House of Worship. When my meditations on the moon close down, I walk home and turn on the TV in time to see Neil Armstrong step off the lander.

I step from man to mankind by driving to Ann Arbor, Michigan, to hear the living blues. The musicians are all black and the audience is all white; no one yells boogie. Magic Sam takes my heart away and breaks it later in the year when he dies; I cry for it. Luther Allison debuts big; Fred Dawkins gets mad at his drummer; Clifton Chenier's zydeco amazes me; Howling Wolf comes out on a scooter; B.B. King jams with Roosevelt Sykes; Robert Lockwood Jr. plays roots back to Robert Johnson; I get sunburned.

Monday there is a beach outing. Donna and Cindy have kids in the water; Rochelle and I have sunbathers up on the sand. I am telling Janet O'Shanna, 16-year-old Down's syndrome girl with one working eye, that she has to either sit with us or join Donna in the water. Janet cocks her head to the good-eye side and just stares at me. I ask, "Would you please put suntan lotion on my back?" Touching is a big part of the positive reinforcements. Volunteer Rochelle says, "Janet, if you don't do it, I will." Janet flips her hand up in the air and runs to the water.

Rochelle applies the lotion and rubs my back; I am looking out over the kids and wake up. She does wear a bikini well. At Shore School, the summer is old enough, so there is no longer a pretense between the staff and the kids. Donna tells me, the kindergarten teacher tells me, the director tells me, and I tell me. *Ask Rochelle out.*

Rochelle has to stay after camp is over so her brother can drive her home. I too stay late to talk to Rochelle. We are alone in a classroom when Virginia, an "educable" grown woman who cleans, comes in. Virginia says to me, "Why don't you take Rochelle out?" My mouth drops open, and I ask, "OK Virginia, where to?" "To a show, you know," she smiles. Rochelle smiles. I try to wait a little while after Virginia leaves so my asking won't seem like Virginia's suggestion. Then it is set; we will go to a show.

Rochelle lives in the Albany Park neighborhood of Chicago. It used to be more Jewish; my father's family lived there. On Saturday I tell my parents that I am going out with "Yes, a nice Jewish girl from Albany Park." My father instantly starts to tell me different routes to drive there. My mother tries to correct him. Street names have changed designations. I slip out under the barrage of directions, as Rochelle steps out of her innocent dresses and tweed skirts into tight jeans. She throws a chain around her waist. The moment I buzz the apartment I see a door fly open on the first landing. I look up and know that I am wrong again. I think she will be shy and quiet. Here is a beautiful bombshell! I think, "Now I am really in over my head. Courage!"

Soon we are happily walking into the big sky that hangs over the corners of Fullerton, Lincoln, and Halsted. We are headed to the Three Penny Cinema to see *Monterey Pop.* Suddenly we run into an old friend of Rochelle's; she calls him Mike the Freak. They hug and kiss, Mike can't talk because a narc named Jake the Jew is after him. He tells us that if anyone approaches us to ask about him just say "some guy named Pete." "You will know this guy is *Jake the Jew* because he carries these!" He pulls out a royal blue matchbook with gold lettering that reads JAKE THE JEW.

We go into the theater, I put my arm around Rochelle and she puts her arm around me and the stereo sound surrounds us. The film is wonderful and makes us drive all over the North Side. She sticks her head and shoulders out the sunroof and yells at people on the streets. We stop in a coffee shop in Evanston and pull into the empty Dyche Stadium parking lot because Rochelle wants to drive the car. Rochelle drives a few circles in first gear and while she is in the driver's seat, we kiss forcefully and passionately. She says, "Umm, that's good!" Next she says, "I hate kissing in parking lots!" We zoom off to a park bench, to my parents' dark living room, back to Albany Park, pull up before her building. Rochelle lies back across my lap, tells me a long story about her high school French teacher. Then she looks up and suddenly tells me to get down. I hunker down below the dash as a short old man totters tipsy up the street past us. When he is gone, we straighten up. "That's my father." We make out more and finally end the date.

Woo the lights all turn green on McCormick Blvd. I am in love with the drag racers that live there after 2 a.m. Rochelle's looks, her short blond hair and hard forceful body, the way she returns love for love, she dazes me for days. Little Bitty and I are all set to hear Crosby, Stills, and Nash on my nineteenth birthday. I feel strange with her now. I can't think of anything to say. We kiss, but we don't want to. "Should I take you home now?" She leans against me as I drive with one arm tightly around her. Standing under her porch light, surrounded by low evergreens, I say I guess things are over and she says she knows it too. We can't figure out why we are not sad. I tell her how another girl has me "all tied up." Jane is relieved to know there won't be an unhappy ending. We kiss one last time, and it is just like the first time.

Next day I fly to Boston to visit cousins. My heart is beating in Chicago. I call long distance to Albany Park to ask for another date. Rochelle and I see each other every day until school starts again. She meets my father on the day my Grandma Esse, his mother, dies. Father is warm and friendly to Rochelle, confusing her but pleasing her too. Father changes in his attitude toward me also. Rochelle is starting college at the University of Illinois at Chicago Circle but still lives at home. I am driving out of Chicago down I-55 to I-80, in a black T-shirt, west to Iowa City, wising up to the blues.

1969 – 1970

Epistolary Year

Iowa City lies along the Iowa River; it is a small town with a university at its core. There are lawns and parks. Oak trees drop acorns as the days shorten. I kick at the leaves and listen to soft sounds of the campus growing dark. I have my own room in a boarding house. I envision Rochelle writing to me. I open my own page.

> It's getting dark
> > > the birds, crickets, and toads
> > are coming out
> the air is soft, fresh even mello
>
> I am very poor at spelling

The student union is close by. I get a coffee and sit in the cafeteria, aka the Pigpen, writing to her. My spelling is nonexistent; I am a medieval scribe. I have complete freedom and don't have to think about how to spell a word when I write. I can only sometimes catch my errors of sight. The mail is a ritual of love. Licking the envelope and affixing the moistened stamp, the pages are folded and slipped in. Chicago to Iowa City takes two or three days. We start to write every day. We don't answer each letter as much as add to an accumulation of dialogue. Misunderstandings take weeks to clear up.

I often see Steve Toth at the student union. I know him from a class. We talk. He quickly tells me he is a poet. This explains why his jacket hangs off him funny and why he keeps a lookout for any half-consumed tray of french fries left on a table. We share some fries and become friends. Steve has a mischievous smile. He has an obscure knowledge of an even more obscure art. He takes me to my first poetry reading: Mark Strand. I love it. I tell Steve so while filing out, and then he says, "There was one good line." Oh, there is so much more to poetry to learn!

> I can go to the beach
> > look at sunsets and stars
> > > maybe a moon
> > I feel like that toward you, also
>
> I pierced my ears today

She pierces her ears. This is exciting. It is as if she is doing this because of us, our letters.

I look forward to them; I know when the mail carrier usually delivers. I sign up for an Understanding Poetry course taught by Phil Dacey. I don't understand how but write poor poetry in my letters.

When I have nothing to do,
        I study and then go sit in the "pigpen"
    I might just go completely straight
Smoking with the 'boys' is just no good

I hope you don't mind my answering so soon

Dacey has a three-page list of poetry books by individual poets. Our assignment is to purchase one of these books. I scour the poetry at the Iowa Book and Supply and decide the best poetry value would be the most poems for the least purchase price. *For Love* by Robert Creeley is my choice. These nubby poems prick my sensitive spots in ways I can't seem to read. I hang on to this volume like stowing a lifesaver for when needed.

If you talk to my mother around her birthday
    see what she says about my note
I sent her a small note that should be a first for my family
    it was simple, sincere, and forthright

I didn't know if I was in love with you
        because I did not know what love was
    but I was learning
I've graduated now!

Willie Dixon sings "I'm Ready." I have thrown down a glove. Will she pick it up? I feel a cloud of urgency. She is 17-years-old. I want my first time to be illegal. Luckily the mail time lag keeps everything at an even pace. Classes can happen. I drive to Chicago every other weekend. We have a whirlwind of dating, then I drive back. On I-80 I pick up hitchhikers who make the trip more interesting. Kids are moving around the country. There is camaraderie post-Woodstock and new pressure to scratch some big itch.

I can't take it here!
    I not only can't stand my father
        but my Mother too —a lot!
everything here is lies!

When I woke up this morning
    I was depressed
I went to see if there was mail
    and I found your letter,
after reading the letter,

> I walked to my bedroom
> closed the door
> grabbed my pillow and screamed into it!

I get a sudden shudder of dread. I am making a mistake. I am falling over in my head. Of course she can't love me. I cannot be loved. I beat myself up calling out sexually demeaning names. There is no love possible without hope of love's return.

> If what I think a mind-fuck is,
> I probably have it now
> I don't love you in a way
> that's passionate and insane
> and all excited
> I love you
> like it's a fact
> example: I have two feet
> that's a fact

I am baffled. I am conditioned to wait and see. This is her glove, more stark than lips can reveal. I pick it up, and she has mine. These gloves don't match, though they betoken union. They may eventually wear down to common threads.

> Now you have "clouds" to tear you up
> Boy, late last night,
> I listened to Joni and thought about you
> and about you
> being mad at me
>
> We can go play in the leaves out somewhere
> I sure could dig building a leaf fort

This is me at my best: *go play*. A universal offer to fix ourselves is nearby in small words; we are fully explored. If love is a matter of fact, I am its naturalist.

I walk along the riverbank; her letters are stuffed in my coat pocket. I need them with me. I fear rejection as the denial of love. I want her stripped down like our letters, incompressible, also shy, afraid to hurt. They are kisses on bumps and lumps. Only in my letters am I hesitant to hold her all night. Asking permission, but when she is inches near there is no stop sign. She doesn't want me to ask permission. She is grounded and long past yessing me.

> I'm sitting in a lounge with a bunch
> of girls I graduated with
> and most are smoking   it's weird

I went to an SDS meeting
    and found myself in an RYMII meeting again
Well you might get mad
    I know you love dirt,
but I washed your hat

Nineteen years a virgin, it seems a nuisance, like having a bloody war in front of me. I am dropping ed. psych as a major. I have no career. I have no answers. I drive to Chicago, and we pretend to know what we are doing.

I think it is good that   crowds don't part for us,
        birds don't sing,
violinists don't follow us

It was a little insane
    how we celebrated
        my grandmother's death
or how people tried to
    push me to take you out

I had funny feelings that it was unmanly
of me to admit that you
    could move me to tears of joy –

statement of fact   like I have two feet

We are both virgins. There is a foreknowledge of a long arc ahead of us. But we can't see it. We only feel it. We have to get it over with quickly and we may as well be sure to break the law while doing it. She turns 18 in January.

I've been reading your letter
over a glass of tea and
    pumpernickel bread
  and cheese
You make me so happy!

I would have enjoyed being kidnapped by you!

Who knows, you may become a good sex partner!
(said kiddingly)

Did you know that our
    spirits secretly leave us at night
        and meet on the bank of the Mississippi?

I imagine the letters on trucks that cross each other while traversing the wide Mississippi. The gray skies fit like a helmet over the horizon. Midwestern longitudes swell under their own weight.

Don't worry about upsetting me
Your "emotional type" letter was so beautiful
I cried. And tears are not
          unmanly! I wish
more men could cry

I don't know what to say
    exactly on staying together, all weekend
It would be
      very good and I'd
like it but I have hang-ups

I can't stand saying things like this in letters

Don't worry about what I said
    about fooling myself about
        loving you

Contradictions are in the song lyrics of my days. Lovers only love for themselves. No one is more selfish than a new lover. I know this somewhere in the bottom of my river. A lover says/does all that is needed to be accepted. I have a tremendous will to please others. I do so selfishly. I know our love is good for us. I ignore her qualms. Who cares? If I am pleasure itself, how can I be hurtful?

If I hurt you
I would be hurting myself

but I would like to spend the night with you
I would hold you all night

    that time you fell asleep
        on top of me   I felt
your warmth, your trust, and your beauty

just as each week
   goes by
this year will go by

I will wait

I say that but waiting is not a target anywhere on my horizon. There is that message again. Just wait. It gets better, the opposite of naturalism. Life does get better if I can just fool myself better too. I see poetry as devoid of ownership, free of the weight of experiences. Each is a natural heft: draft, career, sex.

> Our relationship is quite young
> Later will be too late We have to be honest early
>
> I don't think I can say
>   I love you   now

She comes out on the bus. I sneak her into my cold room. We quietly get under the covers. She is a holy keyhole even if she isn't holy. I plead my pressing desires. The last permission: *I want to touch there. I wish you would.*

> You're probably around Davenport
>
> I'm going crazy
>   the room is silent and empty
>   unless you come back

The leaves are all down. Sidewalks are slippery after cold rains. There is a warm silence to be held in your mother's arms. Counting cars in the middle of the night. Earaches go away in her silent embrace. I sign up for a creative writing class. Graduate student Norman Fischer is encouraging. What does he know? He reads a brilliant Iowa Workshop prose scenario about a man and woman at the breakfast table. The cereal boxes go snap, crackle, and pop.

> Remember Saturday night you
>   said something about
>   someday having the rare privilege
> of making love to me?
> I don't want you to think
>   it's such a rare privilege
> I mean . . .
> I don't want to be put on a pedestal
>
> I will also be making love to you
>
> Maybe I can help fill
>   that empty silence in your room
>
>   It's raining now
>   and very cool
> there should be a lot of leaves
>   on the ground
>   if they're not too wet

The war is at its darkest. The government only lies. The TV news is a 30-minute nightly portal into fear. There is going to be a lottery for the draft. The Radical Students Association holds a teach-in on General Hershey's statement on the purpose of the draft. I learn about societal channeling while being channeled.

It's weird
we both thought of
pedestals at the same time

I never bring up my mail
until the bed is made
the chair set straight   a record on
a cup of coffee   curtains opened   oh yes
and I must be fully dressed
It is like bringing a friend up

I don't like PL much
I'm in the Radical Student Associates
SDS at Iowa is PL
RSA would be similar to RYMII
but not really

I already
miss you so much
my mother made me feel stupid
for wanting to call you
I don't care if I just saw you today!

I'm going to quit SDS
I don't have time or motivation
I'd rather get into Zionism and People and
Children and Art and Music
and feel good

She plays guitar and sings "When I Met You on the Midway". Maybe I don't think heaven is real, nothing is. I know one tangible thing. I start taking myself to poetry readings. Looking for a reality that fits my skin. I hear words, but they play me like a musical instrument. Does the guitar know the song or just fake it?

I'm sitting here alone
in an auditorium
waiting for a poetry reading to begin
the poet is reading

> it is hard to get much out of a poem
> only hearing it once
> I get eager being surrounded by the words
> certain words make me see
> some make me sad
> others make me happy
>
> my world seems new

Here is the palace of words. They come to me in letters. They come in books. They come out of the mouths of professors. I talk to myself. This is my special talk. The talk I can't share but in poetry. I do see words. Nothing else.

> I'm going to have
> to get out of SDS
> I can't take it now
> there's no pleasant way out now, I guess

I am dazed, contemplating going into the army. Girls don't have that problem. I meet a student, a vet, on the GI bill. His dope is narcotic and he is fucked up. My fantasy has always been soldiering. I see no comradeship in this man's army. I know I am not a coward.

> I don't think you know me
> I don't know you
> I can be very terrible sometimes
> I don't know if you can take that in me
>
> today was exciting, I participated in my
> first demonstration

I hear the draft lottery on the radio, breathlessly listening as days of the year are pulled out of a drum. Unfortunately, I don't have to wait long.

> I am 44th on the list
> forever and ever!

> I just found out   You're 44
> I don't feel too well
> If you go to the army
> I'll die

Let's die together first. There is nothing to tether us to on this earth. The snows are melting a little and days are lengthening. Whiffs of spring in January smell like an elixir.

Life is in a bottle. There is only one way out to get it out. I have to tip it over.

I was reading psych

"the desire for sexual gratification, if frustrated,
may be sublimated in the writing of love letters . . ."

then I remembered not only was I
sexually frustrated but also
I had not written you today

this will be my last letter
before I see you

I'll be holding you soon
I'll be seizing you in the same old places

I suddenly stop. Take a look around my old room, the attic in my parents' house; the floor has tough industrial – light green carpeting. No one else is in the house. We each have two feet. For a first time, it seems time stops but the Earth moves.

lover   I really like that

now we are lovers   that sounds nice

now you are my lover
and I am yours
that's good

The road rolls beneath me. Iowa is a supple mound to come back to. Whatever else happens or never happens again, I feel made. Our love needs no future. I apply to University of Illinois, Chicago Circle. Now my draft status is number one as soon as my student deferment ends. I have two more years.

right now you must be asleep

warm and curled up
under that huge fluffy blanket
only the sounds of the radiator
your sister's breathing
are present

you're stronger
than I am now
your letters are necessary

I told my therapist that I'm
          sleeping with you
and that I'm happy I'm doing it
     I also told him that you're more important
               to me than my family
He thought all this was great

The world rests in its orbit. When curtains are drawn, there are new worlds to create. Losing childhood invites acceptance. Now so much more comes into view. I am stronger too. I see myself ready to change by changing awareness.

You're probably moody
          at times because of me
You take too much shit from me
          I often act like an ass
          talk too authoritatively
               that I'm often too cruel
I really like it when you
          put me down
               for treating you like a child

Hell, you would be doing yourself a favor too
          if you pointed these things out!
I really don't want to be an ass!

Winter is lame; it drags its foot over us. It is so long to spring. I sense my life will be starting over. I can't stop thinking about the war. There is a lot of waiting but nothing to see: gray skies, white fields, a drear interstate to everywhere.

I weigh
     95 lbs
          with my clothes on
          and after I have eaten

I called Planned Parenthood
          to change my appointment
     they asked my name
          then my husband's name
I told them   I didn't have one

Weather forecast is more teach-ins about the war. Nixon is not ending the war. He talks about eliminating all deferments. I am slipping in my classes. This might hurt my GPA. Relevancy is a heavy coat I am sliding out of. Teachers are annoying. They add useless classwork on top of my worries. I am bandaged together by our letters.

we went up into the old
Capitol
lounged around
on the senate tables
sat around in windows
as if we had taken
the place over

Nixon dropped occupational
deferments and
student deferments later

I guess Canada
may look pretty
certain very soon

I am alone. My family is a thousand cornfields away. My friends now seem to be into poetry. I don't know where that is. Where will I live? Am I a coward? When I think poetry is one thing, it becomes another. Jerome Rothenberg reads from *Technicians of the Sacred*. Shape shifting voices rise up from the frozen ground. The first Earth Day is April 22, 1970.

I went to a couple of teach-ins
for Earth Day
it would seem a sin
to bring a baby
into this doomed planet

baby will
later curse you
for his black lungs

I just turned my clocks ahead

It's almost May; snow is melting, leaving the gross aspects of life struggling to adjust.

tomorrow I'm not
going to school
I'm striking
against Cambodia   and
those dead students
ROTC too
I'm striking
about everything   I think is wrong

There is a commotion at the women's dorms; a huge number of male students have crossed the river and stand below demanding underwear. I am observing the yearly ritual; a guy yells out that U.S. troops are firing on students in Ohio. Killing them. Women come down; all of us go to the Pentacrest, the center lawn between the oldest campus buildings. SDS leaders struggle to gain control. We are an unruly mob that attacks the bookstore windows.

right now they are trying
            to break down
        the doors to Old Cap.

Politically I feel confused
Physically I am a wreck

the kids don't have
            their heads together
or
their politics straight
                yet

I'll stand in the street
        I won't throw rocks

We forced the cancellation
    of Governor's Day

        We were out
    on the Pentacrest all night
        it was too cold

A band played
        they took a collection
    and bought dope
        for everyone

today busloads of
        Nat'l Guardsmen
            with short guns
    were brought in

State cops with guns, too

            Army helicopters overhead

    maybe they will shut
        down school early

I hope Nixon

doesn't goof up

Tonight or tomorrow

or else

everything could blow up

I love you

the pigs won't stop that!

We huddle in Chicago as the world upheaves around us. Making love is a casual sport. Odd moments in parent front rooms. We understand each other. My favorite part of driving is crossing the Mississippi River. It is so big that the interstate cannot dwarf it. The air is moist; it penetrates the many ways we steal ourselves.

I marched to the

Behavioral Science Building

we blocked and picketed

every entrance

it happened all over campus

they closed Kent for the spring

Campuses are still active

and rioting and demonstrating

In New York, construction

workers beat up student

demonstrators

they asked Lindsay

to have the flag half-mast

at City Hall

he agreed

the workers wanted it up

my Dad tried to get

hold of the White House

the president

or one of his advisers

he was a little drunk

and mad at everyone at home

he wanted to tell

the president

to shoot all the demonstrators

he was telling the operator
he had some important
advice
I went to my room
and just fell apart

Oh, god. My grades are shit. The school is closing early. Students have a choice. Grades will be given from the midsemester point or classes will be offered again. I take my grades.

the place is quiet now
even though

campus buildings
are crawling
with riot police
police with high powered rifles

No one can study

this will be my last
letter to you

I could be home
by the time you read this

I'm a bit packed now

maybe I'm holding you now

perhaps by now
we have even
broken through
the small barriers
time and distance
put between us

1970 – 1973

The Proposal

> ". . . rejoicing in a peace which only
> brings an increase of anxiety, and in
> a prosiness which serves as a deep
> source of poetry to the stranger who
> passes through their midst without
> having lived among them."
>
> – Marcel Proust, *Swann's Way*

Who cuts your fine figure? Who makes me move to Chicago? I grow up on the North Shore, always long to get out of the safe green scenery and into the tough nut Chicago. During High School, I volunteer to teach reading skills to black fourth graders in Lawndale, the West Side neighborhood. I learn a lot. Our yellow bus full of pudgy white faces attracts green-tinted coke bottles that fly into the windows, spraying us with glass. This adds a firm base to our understanding of just who is teaching whom. It isn't for them; I go. What could I do for them? No, it is for me. For me that Chicago exists now. Rochelle lives in it and I am returning to her. Chicago is the hometown of my parents; the bluesy place of my birth; a fresh breeze from Fort Dearborn, built in a stinking onion patch.

During the summer, we hunt for separate apartments. After seeing a place on Dayton Street, we have our first fight. I mention Sophia Loren. Rochelle asks, "Would you sleep with Sophia Loren?" With some hesitation, I answer her after thinking that each earthworm has both sex organs yet it still takes two worms to reproduce, all four sexes! "Of course I would!" Rochelle turns red. Speechlessly mad. This becomes the pattern. I pick up Rochelle at her parents house; within a few blocks, we are fighting. I start to wonder why I transferred to University of Illinois, Chicago Circle. I tell Rochelle that I have *wanderlust*, a dangerous word to introduce into any relationship. A terrible anxiety is created. I take the apartment on Dayton Street near Armitage, and she moves onto Wisconsin Street, which is very close to Lincoln Park. A month after classes at UI Circle start, we break up.

There is so much need built in that we know each other too well for the amount of time we actually spend together. Why hadn't we met a year or two later? Rochelle is undergoing stress: leaving her parents house, finding cockroaches in her new apartment, first time living with roommates. I am feeling sorry for myself for leaving my friends in

Iowa City and moving to a big city where I know only one person. Instead of enjoying upperclassman comforts at Iowa, I am a bumbling new student looking up at signs over doors to find my classroom.

Circle is a commuter school, students are seen waiting for buses or squeezing onto the el platform. It is hard to met new people. We are walking up Wells Street to see an art movie down an ally to our left. I make a classist crack to her. Instead of turning down the alley, Rochelle keeps walking straight. She wants me to call out to her; I fool myself. But I don't because I think I am being the stronger of the two. I doubly fool myself. I soon want Rochelle back after our split-up. I am only *strong* for a few weeks.

I reread Robert Creeley's *For Love*. The poems sound through space into my life. "The Warning" shocks me into wanting Rochelle back even if it splits my head open. I am aware of Rochelle's old suitor who reappears. I renew my quest for her love; I head over to Wisconsin Street early in the afternoon and ask Rochelle to walk through Lincoln Park with me. She makes me wait four hours while she irons her clothes in the kitchen. Her roommate enjoys my obvious distress. At last, Rochelle consents to go outside with me; she hates her roommate worse than she does me.

We walk through the late afternoon autumn lake breezes and kick tawny leaves that swirl along the path. Lake Michigan swells up into big fluffy waves; we start to run holding hands. Under the arch of Ulysses S. Grant, strangers kiss. That is it. Cut back to her bedroom as windows turn black nighttime.

I have to know about her boyfriend. I have to ask, and I do. "I didn't do anything I wouldn't do with you." She sweetly smiles. I piss in my intestines. Renewed love smashed to nothing. I flee her to go through this alone. Grab the rails on the stairwell of Big Irony. I too had a girlfriend, but at bedtime, I can only think about Rochelle. You can't make love to one person while thinking of another; somebody always gets hurt. I feel virtuous. Rochelle looks so accommodating. I am a prude and an idiot! Where else do I think my talk of wanderlust and being free lead? Just so, the absurdity of life dumps on my head.

Less resolved, I have pure love and something less. Now the twists of Creeley's pitchfork fully turn me inside out. Swallowed pride must stay swallowed. Rochelle and I remain a couple and school continues. Living the blues, I start to come alive to my surroundings. Every street ends in the lake. On the corner of my block at Armitage stands a church converted into the national headquarters of the Young Lords. Portraits of Che Guevera and Lolita Lebron grace the stone church walls. The block has modest three-story buildings and is an easy walk to the Lincoln Park Zoo.

I go to the zoo often and rejoice in the true social dynamics found there. The animals have to perform their animal chores while a steady stream of other animals toss peanuts and marshmallows. Poke fun. Stare. There are regulars who attend to their special animals behind bars. They discuss the behavior and health of their animals. To the animal in the cage, these vagabond gods prove their own existence. Love exists in the bars between us.

Broadway is also close by with its theaters, The Body Politic and Kingston Mines. Several well-known watering holes round out the immediate neighborhood: Wise Fools Pub, John Barleycorn, Red Baron. Three Penny Cinema and Biograph Theater are near by at Fullerton and the Bryn Mawr Cinema's 50-cent-movies are a few el stops uptown. Belmont Beach is an easy walk.

Midwest summer balloons before us; Rochelle and I plan to open up my grandfather's cottage in northern Wisconsin. I am still shaky about our relationship. I have a frightful feeling of impurity and loss of territorial integrity. I am not yet 21. I display a sexual martyrdom voiced through macho masochism. As I take the large whitewashed shutters off the Russian cottage, I get a strong feeling that Rochelle and I will split up again.

Luckily, Steve Toth, who introduced me to poets at Iowa, comes up to celebrate my birthday. We have a series of talks on smoky topics. At first the range of the talk seems ponderous, but as we continue the discourse Steve disarms my preconceived notions about everything. He teaches me how not to define God in my thoughts. "Don't make God fit you." This release makes my life fit God. Steve's shy smile triggers a key in the door that opens to my body center. He also teaches me about tequila on my twenty-first birthday. Immediately after our farewells, I walk into the woods to sit. After several empty days, I go back into the cabin. The wind blows off the lake; it blows through the cabin; it blows through the trees; – until the wind is broken, diverted into breezes, then nothing. I don't feel a thing. I don't hear a thing, must be a thing, is a thing. Thing walks into the cabin; thing writes a poem. Thing knows everything. Thing writes the last line: *I will leave my rusty cabbage by the lake.*

Poems come from a new place. They sing a bit and bounce a bit and they do something real. I realize that I can be a writer. The giant weight of career falls from my shoulders. I understand that I can go through life being somebody rather than owning something. I don't have to buy into the corporate fantasy of happiness. I am on a sure path to find myself, ready to look at love all over again.

I see my physical world in words. Without actually seeing words, poetry sings word rhythms into my ears. The dangerous cycles that seek to break up Rochelle and me vanish. I see a beautiful young woman across the red-checkered tablecloth on the porch. I am grateful to have the chance to meet Rochelle again. Naively happy, I am relieved at commencing the impossible task of being a poet lover true. Rochelle is busy being Rochelle. I see that she is not embroiled in the tragedy I play for myself in our love. I simply become more agreeable. We are planning to share my apartment; now my fears are allayed. We return to Chicago and set up house on Dayton Street; things seem easy for us. Rochelle's father remarks, "It's about time."

We fix up the apartment and find that the convenience of living together allows us the time and freedom to be apart. Our bedroom is a converted back porch with an inadequately heated western view. The room sticks out into the sky; we are often bathed in direct moonlight as we sleep. I get nosebleeds simultaneously with Rochelle getting her period. These are our moon nights.

The living room is funky: stage scenery saguaro cactus, stuffed frog mariachi playing a guitar, doorways to hall, kitchen porch. Down the hall is a tiny second bedroom oddly dominated by a huge hanging crystal chandelier. Getting downtown to Circle campus means catching the Halsted Street bus at Armitage. The twenty-minute bus ride lurches past the Cabrini-Green housing projects, Skid Row, Greek Town; arrives at the newly constructed bi-level modular Circle Campus.

The Vietnam War dispenses death to all in its path. I have my senior year left to figure out some kind of crazy route out of serving; after all my father being a psychoanalyst, I should be nuts. In the fourth and fifth grades, I was sent to a pediatric psychiatrist. Now it may be useful. I see a young psychiatric colleague of my father's. He is willing to interview me and write a letter. This letter portrays me as a terrible mess. More ammunition. He recommends a different psychoanalyst for me to see on a regular basis.

Dr. Ernest Wolfe has an office downtown in the ornate Pittsfield Building. We start on a psychotherapeutic basis. I sit up and we talk to each other. I let him know how happy I am with my girlfriend and my passion for poetry. My talk about the creative process intrigues him. He suggests we switch to the psychoanalytic model with me lying down, talking without seeing him listening. I will come more often. but the price drops a little; my Dad is paying. From the prone position on the couch, there is little visual stimulation. The burden is on me to talk. If I am silent, there is only silence. Late into the hour, Wolfe might interject with a recap of my talk. This prompts me to investigate more deeply. At times, I talk about writing poetry. Since I know nothing about it, I am processing a great number of ideas at once. Wolfe is well read and I use character metaphors from literature. I am reading *Moby Dick* again in class. A great white whale swims within me. As I ramble, I sometimes trigger a nearness to a deep leviathan issue I can only feel the surface of. It overwhelms me. I begin to understand that analysis takes years to open up the entire psyche. The analytical meetings are a great comfort to me because I can now properly understand psychoanalytic terms my father misapplied to me when I was little. He called me Little Oedipus, Schizophrenic, and even Psychoneurotic. Maybe this is why my father complains about having to pay my shrink bills.

I look around for a way to express my new bent towards poetry. I take Paul Carroll's poetry writing workshop. Paul leads a friendly group where each member gets to read a poem after which he offers mild encouragement, "I admire the energy in that!" He assigns his anthology *The Young American Poets*, which turns out to be an excellent selection of poets a generation older than us. Paul's first assignment is to go to the Art Institute and write about De Chirico's *The Philosopher's Conquest*. As I stand staring at the green sky, the artichokes, the train puffing off to the horizon, a fellow with long brown hair and a goatee says, "Hi." He too is on Paul's assignment. Peter Kostakis invites me to another poetry writing workshop in the Alternate University at Circle. He explains that the poets meet once a week and offer honest criticism with no assigned leader.

A dozen poets sit around the table. One hands out copies of their poem and then reads it. The reaction is swift. The poem is critiqued on word choice, vagueness, line arrangement; wholesale deletions are recommended. I am shocked and relieved I have no poem with me. There are no experts. Each workshop member offers serious observations. I am intrigued enough to want this same close attention. Several poets stand out to me. Peter is here, and there is Richard Friedman, who talks a lot and seems friendly. A woman with dark hair and deep eyes, Darlene Pearlstein, also dominates the poetry discussion. After the workshop, Richard and Darlene walk out together, an obvious couple. There is also Richard's red-haired buddy Deeds (Don Nisonoff) and Barry Schecter, rubbing a villainous mustache are there.

I go next week with copies of my poem, get my first dose of harsh criticism. The savagery of poets' advice doesn't rescue a poem but it has a beneficial impact on the next poem. – "Oh, I can't write this because Richard will say it is too anemic." A critical apparatus which operates on the lines before they strike the page, starts to creep into my head.

Richard and Darlene invite Rochelle and me to their apartment on New Year's Eve 1971. Peter is here too. Richard, Peter, and I arm wrestle until Rochelle and Darlene fall asleep on the bed. Peter goes home after midnight. Richard and I stay up talking until dawn. We both grew up on the North Shore. We graduated sister snooty high schools. However Richard's story is more filmic than my urban tutoring. He took lots of drugs, got busted for distributing LSD, and landed in the nuthouse. Richard's story moves me, makes me jealous of his perfect poet background. Something new rises in my life. Suddenly, Richard is my bosom friend. I need new friends and Richard is a natural writer. Everything he writes sounds good; he is able to write powerful poems that have political and personal impact. He knows more about poetry than I do.

Peter and I also form a friendship through poetry. He too is ahead of me in knowledge and ability. His poetry is strongly surreal and mostly outrageously funny. Darlene is high on her own opinions that filter into her well-crafted rhymed children's poetry. Deeds is Richard's high school friend who writes sharply clever poems; his ambition is to become a sports writer. Barry is the sixth writer in our group. He is the eldest, which cloaks him in mystery. He embodies Kafka. Barry's poetry is delicate and enduring. We start to draw closer into a poet cabal in both the Alternate and in Paul Carroll workshops. We support each other and teach each other.

I lie down for Dr. Wolfe around the noon hour. I take the el from Circle to the Loop, then back again for afternoon classes. I am standing on the platform waiting for a train, studying the sharp lines marking the dark area near the tracks and the band of light cement below the blue sky above the opposite platform. The sharp visual distinctions start to swirl in my face. I know that if I am home with a notebook, I am writing a poem. I extend the swirling pre-poem aura into the Loop and up to Wolfe's office. I talk and talk rapid fire about art and creativity and abstract geometric formulations to hold it all together. I talk straight through the hour. Wolfe tells me later that although hard to follow, it deeply intrigues him.

Going through my childhood backward eases my relations with my father. I can see him and things he says as just being a part of him. Wolfe lets me understand that all thought is permissible but all thoughts do not need to be acted on. I stop trying to force Rochelle to conform to my cultural expectations. The longer I am in psychoanalysis, the surer I become of my own mental soundness.

How else am I going to get out of the draft? I am managing an ugly case of deep cystic acne. Luckily the sores are on my chest and back, easy to hide. I treat them with a strong acid gel from my dermatologist, who went to medical school with my father. This acid ointment is supposed to be applied twice a week. I start to apply it daily. The dermatologist secretly tells me he will diagnose eczema, a surefire 4-F. Eczema entails a lifetime of care, and the Army doesn't want the added medical expense. As my skin blisters, I keep appointments with the doctor to build up a case for the treatment of eczema.

The isle of Manhattan is the center of Richard's poetry talk. This place is the seat of literary activity for the nation and beyond. He regales me about the New York School poets. I imagine a Gothic revival setting like the University of Chicago; – poets teaching in fetching garb among ivy walls. Richard shows me this place for real in his well-turned copy of Donald Allen's *The New American Poetry anthology*. He tells me one of the New York School's greatest champions is coming to Chicago to teach at Northeastern Illinois University. Richard says, "We will meet Ted Berrigan!"

Ted Berrigan's poem "Tambourine Life" changes Richard's and Deed's lives. In Paul Carroll's workshop, we read *Tambourine Life* out loud in a roundrobin. The poem, with its brilliant upswings and devastating breakdowns, brings me to secret tears as it closes:

69

What moves me most, I guess
         of a sunlit morning
    is being alone
        with everyone I love
crossing 6th and 1st
at ice-cold 6 a.m.

    from where I come home
      with two French donuts, Pepsi and
        the New York Times.

70

    Joy is what I like,
    That, and love.

What a mysterious place 6th and 1st is! The entire weight of the poem comes to bear on this location. Berrigan's distance home is now short. Simple pleasure, antic and accepted love, uncontained joy flows out. I begin to get glimmerings of how to simplify my lines and amplify their effect.

Ted Berrigan is replacing Ed Dorn at Northeastern University and living in Dorn's Diversy Street house. Dorn is very influential and has engendered a group of poets at the college. They come to Paul's workshop en masse to read their poems. They talk about a cryptic circuit. The bell rings just as Steve Pantos begins a poem. Everyone starts to slip on coats. Steve looks up and scowls, "You better sit down; this will take a while." Everybody does, and it does take a while. They publish a poetry magazine called *Stone Wind*. Steve Pantos, Terry Jacobus, Al Simmons, and Henry Kanabus; we refer to them as the Stone Wind poets. They employ the enigmatic sharp line from Dorn; deliver their poems with drunken staccato scraped off the streets of Chicago. Like the streets of Chicago, they make sense. The Stone Wind gang is not in evidence in Ted's workshop.

I miss the first meeting of Ted's workshop, but the reports fascinate me. Darlene says, "Oh, he is terrible! He said that there are no such things as images! What a big ego! He is really awful!" Richard is more reserved and careful around Darlene. I can tell he enjoys the workshop. The next week I go and start a complimentary poetry education to the severe attacks of the Alternate Circle workshop. Ted brings copies of the mimeographed *World* magazine from the Poetry Project and orders everybody to subscribe to it. I do. Ted presents the world of poetry and how to find it even in this makeshift classroom in back of an art gallery on Bryn Mawr Avenue. He addresses the reader in us as he talks. I wonder how he can talk for so long in a manner that teeters between ennui and inspiration. This is poetry in the deep end; it keeps students in their seats with their minds slightly reeling. Ted offers an entire vocabulary to discuss the mechanisms of poetry. Poetry books start to flood into my puny library.

Berrigan sparks our Circle group to get busy on campus. We decide to request funds from the student government to publish an anthology of the Alternate Circle

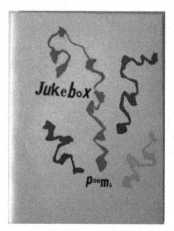

workshop and request funds to offer Ted a reading at Circle. Both requests come through. Rochelle is busy studying Medieval Art History, and making her own new friends. But there is crossover; she likes to sit in our poetry sessions. Her spark and sprightliness is an asset to our group and we include her. After Ted's reading at circle, it is Rochelle who presents him with the check. He takes it and asks, "What is your name?" "Rochelle Kraut." "Kraut! You get more interesting all the time." Darlene elbows me, "Ted likes Rochelle."

Our anthology is coming out. We call it *Jukebox Poems,* and Rochelle designs the cover.

The group of poets I run with edit ourselves

in, to the exclusion of those poets who are only peripheral members of the Alternate workshop. This results in bad feelings that deliver a death blow to the openess of the workshop. With the anthology out and the resultant criticisms behind us, the workshop becomes less necessary to us now.

> January 20, 1972
> Dear Editor,
>
> I don't know how I've managed to miss your mag until recently! I've always written in secret (my parents are religious fanatics who only read the Bible. Other literature to them belongs to the devil because God only wrote one book.) When I saw *Circula* for the first time, I realized that I must express myself (even if it means going to hell). I'm submitting to your critical eyes a piece I did concerning a view on life from a modern Jewish mystic. I'm not Jewish myself, but I feel poetry can transcend even major cultural differences. I plan to keep my door locked and my only path in the mainstream of life open by sending you more of my works in the future.
>
> Sincrely,
> Derek Steele

Distance Makes Corned Beef Grow Fonder

Pass the mustard, I'm
Writing a poem.
Which reminds me:
I've been meaning to speak to you
About your father
In the bagel factory
Endlessly folding away bagels
into the (rather human) night.
Delightful as a wonderland of yellow paper,
He stands – marked
With trepidation, touching the skin
Of a future onion roll, thinking
Of you.
In the bakery endlessly rolling
Jelly rolls,
On into the night (still human form).
If Ashkenaz only could know
The patriarchal pain that

Rends their pastry,
They'd writhe into miles of
Mustard-yellow spastic light.

Derek Steele

Derek Steele is the invention of Barry Schechter and myself. We have exclusive rights to his existence and keep him a strict secret from Peter and Richard. *Circula* is a lame newsprint arts publication put out by the Circle student government. It infuriates us all with its horrible student poetry selections. Barry and I conspire to get published in it under our pseudonym. We set upon the difficult task of writing intentionally bad poetry. The poem above is our first attempt to get published. Our second attempt succeeded with only slightly less obnoxious poems: *My Grandmother O.D.-ed* and *Once I Saw an Old Man*. You should hear Richard yowl when that issue hits the free bins. What surprises me most about Derek is how much Wolfe is interested in him. I try to figure out why Derek perks up his analytic ears so. Is it that an artist is already a foil of the artist's self and so the art of an imaginary artist is somehow more real? More revealing?

While Derek continues to write poems, everyone else is writing their own. Peter prepares absolutely outrageous ditto packages with collages of cutouts and his own poems:

EL GRABADO

Beneath the nudity
of the moon
I learn of my wedding
to distance

To amaze the veins
deltas exploded on the pale hand
like guns that do not fire
– that is what is expected of me

Beneath the nudity
of the moon
I imitate stone

Peter Kostakis

Peter has a touch of the eternal in his approach. Richard takes a bite out of the here and now to good effect over a fuller page as his long poem ends:

> Straight overhead,
>
>   the ceiling has rolled down
>   into the walls
>   like subway doors
> & the night's
>   navy blue background
>
>   outlines
>
>   thousands
>
>   of brilliant
>
>   silver
>
>   constellations
>
>   Richard Friedman

I am ready for a breakthrough. Ted suggests that we should read James Schuyler's poetry. I purchase Schuyler' *Freely Espousing* in a second-hand bookstore in Hyde Park. Schuyler's domestic tough voice is an immediate knock on my door. I write a poem, "The Affirmative Statement"; free of surreal thickness, the poem is about inhabiting poetry. It ends with these lines:

> many letters arranged
> in my coat pocket
> along with the poems of James Schuyler
> this time everything remains stationary
> until I walk across
> or tell you so

Schuyler shows me how to allow a soft stirring of air into my cadence.

Richard and Peter decide to start a poetry magazine to be published by what will be called: The Yellow Press. Darlene is instantly offended. Our group has an understanding to start a magazine together as a group of editors. Richard, for his love of Darlene, and Peter, for his love of peace, give in and the magazine becomes *our* project. Since both Richard and Peter are guilty of having a good idea, neither volunteers to be the first editor. Darlene also refuses, so I am elected. We call it The Milk Quarterly; milk is at once pure, pregnant, pernicious, and both noun and verb! The odd part is that we have no plans to bring out an edition four times a year. We love the pun. We add a special "milk" quotation to the endpaper of each issue.

I don't know my cousin Paul Sills (founder of the Second City theater group), but I do know his niece, my cousin Claire. Claire is conducting movement workshops at The Body Politic Theater on Lincoln Avenue. They have a seldom-used mimeograph machine that we can use. It takes hours just to get a first impression down on paper. I tinker with the machine and we print the first issue in the meanest manner. For the second issue, we find a better mimeo and make contacts with poets we like around the country for new poems. We receive the usual Chicago critique. "What does this got to do with Chicago?" The Yellow Press is committed to being a national press.

Within Chicago, there is a fierce sense of rivalry that pervades social groups and cultural self-worth. It stems from the Second City syndrome: A. J. Liebling writes widely misunderstood articles in *The New Yorker* about Chicago Ladies who train to New York to shop dresses. Liebling appreciates Chicago's power in unashamed original architecture. There is no need for Chicago to feel slighted by New York. However, my parents remember the articles as being dismissive of Chicago, and the rivalry is hot in Chicago. Chicago is Catholic-flavored; the way New York is flavored Jewish. Chicago fiercely resists and then forgives the new.

We talk about the Stone Wind guys and they call us the Milkmen. Over there are the Oinkers (yes! Oink magazine): Paul Hoover, Jim Leonard, and Dean Faulwell, later Maxine Chernoff, conspire at Columbia College Chicago. The Stone Wind guys start a poetry reading series in the basement of an antique store called The Blue Store. It has a musty clubhouse atmosphere. All the boys bring booze to share with their girlfriends and the featured readers. I bring a flask of bourbon and pass it across the gangland lines.

Shelley

> I saw you first in half-darkness
> by candlelight two round table tops away
> sitting in perfect attention with perfect self-awareness
> waiting, for the poetry to begin, in The Blue Store;
> I accepted a drink from your companion's surprising flask,
> never taking my eyes off of you, radiant nineteen-year old,
> and thought, as I was losing my heart,
> "Jesus, there's obviously a lot more to Bob Rosenthal
> than meets the eye?" . . .

Ted Berrigan

The readings are really good. Berrigan brings in poets such as Anselm Hollo, Jim Carroll, Kenward Elmslie, and Dick Gallup. At the open readings, Ted gets up and reads a few of his very best works to bowl everyone over. More poets not quite affiliated with any of the already formed poetry gangs start to appear. Neil Hackman (aka Ravi Singh) frequents the readings. Simon Schuchat comes up from the University of Chicago; Art Lange, John Paul, Alan Axelrod, Jim Feast, and who else? We sit in the dark cellar, soaking up fresh poetry.

Ted often mentions that his wife is "a great poet!" His workshop is where I see Alice Notley for the first time. She is sitting in the back corner, pregnant, tilting back a bottle of Gallo Burgundy. I am prudishly shocked that this Dickensian slum-wench writes poetry. Then Alice reads with Richard at the Blue Store; once again my ears are opened to new dimensions of seeing and believing. Alice reads her sonnet sequence, *165 Meeting House Lane*. The sonnets' lyric honesty and toughness impress me so much I instantly become shy of her.

Ted is drawn to Richard's writing and makes no secret of it. He likes Deeds for quick wit and shared sports knowledge. It isn't until Ted needs someone with a car to help him run off Alice Notley's magazine, *Chicago*, that he turns to me. Richard tells him that I am a mimeo genius and have wheels. I help transport the paper and help print the legal sized magazine. It is a hot day and sweltering in a church mimeo room. Ted takes his pants off. Rochelle drops by with her friend, Sandy. Ted is getting more interesting to us even in his briefs. Ted encourages us to drop in evenings at their house on Diversey Street, which we do. None of my new poetry friends are into getting high. Both Richard and Darlene have already burned themselves out and committed their bodies to the straight and narrow. Peter doesn't need drugs. I mention to Ted that my father is a medical doctor and his eyes bug out.

I never take pharmaceuticals for highs. Primarily, I like grass, liquor, and psychedelics. I ask Ted what are the fun pills to take. Ted tells me that there is a fun pill called Quaalude. I look into my Father's medicine chest and find an unopened bottle. When next I see Ted; I have a few Quaaludes in hand. Cheers. Soon I am rubber legged and giddy. Ted sends me across the street for Pepsi and Chesterfield Kings. I can't believe I am walking, and I am sure that I don't look like I am walking but I get to the store and amazingly find my way back to the house. The first time is always the most remarkable. I drive home and vow if I make it home safe, I will never make this mistake again. Ted is a kind and brusque teacher, and I become a generous supplier.

My senior year is coming to a close. The sudden influx of activity makes life a rich soup. I hardly have time to dream my dreams for Dr. Wolfe. It annoys me that he interprets each dream to be about the analysis or himself. In the spring, I start to write small poems while traveling to and from school on the Halsted Street bus. After a month, I select the good ones and type them up. Richard and Darlene encourage me to put them out as a book. The first Yellow Press book of poetry comes into being: *Morning Poems*.

> I took it easy
> for a moment
> I heard Rochelle fixing breakfast
> somewhere inside me

> *

> In Wisconsin, I take my coffee
> down to the pier
> carefully place it beside me
> and forget about it

The books are about two by three inches to accommodate the short poems. The covers are hand printed by Rochelle and me using potatoes.

I spend $16 on production and sell it for 25¢ each. I make my investment back. With a pleasant book of poetry out and impending challenges of writing and letters, I face the dilemma that has worried me since 1963.

Spring 1972, I get my induction notice. First stop; physical exam. I assemble all my shrink letters. I go back to Evanston and see my old pediatric psychiatrist. It is totally spooky to be back in his office; all I can think about is the tub of candy in the closet. He provides me with a factual statement of my therapeutic time with him. I also have the dire letter from my father's associate that says I beat Rochelle and a letter from Dr. Wolfe that I am currently under his care. I also have a privileged trump card, the letter from the dermatologist.

Thus armed, I arrive early in the morning on the appointed day for my physical. It is held in an old gray warehouse west of the Loop. I am marching up the steps to my own gibbet. A bedraggled bunch of young men are sitting at desks. We take a written test and get talked to by a sergeant. He cynically says, "Many of you will be getting out of doing your service due to your problems." Most of us are clutching letters and looking sick. Then we are handed different colored cards that indicate doctors, Dr. Green, Dr. Yellow, etc. and are told to line up to see civilian doctors who will examine our letters and us. As I shuffle in line for my color, I overhear a different-color doctor yell at a kid, "You can't do this! You sound like a vision of hell! Concentrate on one problem and you'll do better." This kid checked off every ailment on the sheet to the most severe degree: acute insomnia, malignant hangnail, chronic dizziness. My civilian M.D. just glances over my letters without giving any clue as to their validity. After the commonplace taking of specimens, testing of eyes, and less common stretching of ass cheeks, it is late morning before we reach the military doctors. My anxiety is mounting to a fever pitch.

We break into lines divided by flimsy partitions; these lines move very slowly. When I get to his desk and hand him my papers, he scans them quickly then looks up at me sharply, "How do you get along?" "What?" "It says here you are a psychoneurotic mess, and I want to know how you get along?" He is barking. Reminds me of my father, so I dig into a stand and stammer out, "I get along fine." He glares at me some more, but he has to send me to examinations by the civilian specialists called for in my letters. He shoves my letters back to me; I turn around and walk straight into the partition, almost knocking it over. "Follow the yellow tape!" he snarls.

I walk looking down to follow the yellow tape on the floor. It leads me to the shrink's office. The waiting area is lifeless green; old brown school desks litter it. Several of us psychos sit at different angles to one another. During this wait, I start to realize that I am hallucinating. While everyone else is gearing up to act crazy, I am desperately trying to hang on to sanity. When my name is called, I fly out of my seat. The doctor is young and friendly. He too asks me how am I doing. "I'm doing fine!" I shoot back through clenched teeth. The dermatology exam is quick. Then it is over. It seems the lines have gone away and I am the only one left. I approach the checkout desk; the sergeant and his clerk make it clear that the shrink stuff only gives me a one-year deferment but the dermatology exemption lasts a lifetime. The sergeant leans over and says, "You will never be eligible to serve in any of the armed services or." The clerk sardonically interrupts, "He knows that!"

I nod in agreement and walk out the door. The elation I expect is not there; the sky seems empty and sad. Everybody knows about the war in 1972! I notice that all the young men are getting deferred, except for a few clearly clueless ones. Within a year, the entire Selective Service is disbanded. So my one-year deferment would have been enough. There is no relief from being disheartened by the morbid dejection of each person in the induction center. Maybe I would be less shell-shocked if I had simply gotten a higher lottery number.

The Blue Store readings are ending and the Milkmen start a new series. It immediately occurs to me to locate the series at the Body Politic; dark-night Mondays are open to our use. Again I get to be test pilot. Terry Jacobus and I are the first reading; all systems work well. We start scheduling in earnest for the fall. No surprise we want to open the season with Ted. But, who gets to read with him?

Ted suggests Simon Schuchat. *What?* – this hotshot kid from University of Chicago! We have to choose one of us. To be fair to one another, we chose our gang member who is not pretending to be a poet. Rochelle protests, "I don't even write poems!" "No matter," we assure her. Rochelle has her name on many collaborations, so we encourage her to read them without naming the collaborators. I even write a few new poems for her voice. There is a big audience and Rochelle's reading is radiant. She is poised, easy to hear, and funny. I fall for her again in many new ways. Her manner and buoyancy make her poems work. Ted is well-pleased and amused. Later, he tells us that Rochelle "set me up perfectly."

Ted gives a beautiful long reading filled with our requests: "Heroin, "Things to do in Providence," and a second set of just poems from The *Sonnets*. The reading series is successfully launched and becomes popular. We don't pay readers; also don't collect contributions. Peter, Richard, and I take turns preparing introductions that often rival the work of the readers; they are not long, yet they are *off the wall*. I introduce Ed Dorn with some whimsy. Ed gets up and ridicules my introduction before starting. I can't recall what he says because it smarts so much.

I finish college with a degree in American literature. Rochelle has one year left. I have a new love for Melville. I cast about for a job and get one in shipping and receiving for a small music-publishing house. Poetry more and more comes through my door. The poet Bill Knott moves in. Bill needs a cheap place to live so Rochelle and I offer the little room with the chandelier. It is perfect for Bill, who spends all day and night shut into it, composing lines of poetry with a tiny television on. Sometimes he comes out in the evening to let us know that the world's greatest movie is on and then slouches back to his television. We warm up our TV to watch *Straightjacket* with Joan Crawford or other B-movies like the one in which Roddy McDowall is tortured by a starlet. Bill finds the most wonderful bad movies, the very best.

Bill and I occasionally frequent the corner Polish sausage joint. These fat dogs come with onions, jalapeños, half-sour pickle, and a generous helping of french fries that leak grease through the paper bags as we carry them back home.

One evening Ted and Alice come over. Ted calls Bill out of his room; Bill makes one of his rare appearances in the living room. Alice has her baby Anselm George Berrigan with her. Bill politely asks her if she is worried about sudden infant death syndrome. Alice is deeply shocked; she has not yet heard of SIDS. She can't forgive Bill until Anselm outgrows the danger.

After working for five months in the music warehouse, the routine starts to get to me. I am made head of shipping the first week. There is nothing ever new. I am starting to drink lunch at the Billy Goat Tavern. I take some acid and have a good time until I think of going back to work the next day. I get the horrors. I tell Richard about the trip and he tells me that he is Captain Trips and that my horror means I should instantly quit my job. It is sage advice and I take it. I tell Bill that I am quitting and he gets a dismayed paternal look on his face, "Bob, but what are you going to do now?"

It is true. I have to face it. Soon Rochelle graduates. I have no job. Analysis is slowly deescalating in the wake of my draft deferment. I am writing, have loads of friends who also write, *The Milk Quarterly* is pretty good, the Body Politic is a wholesale hit. Richard and I speak every day to share random thoughts; every moment seems accounted for. Young professionals wearing white tennis outfits are moving onto our block and the rents are going up. Both Rochelle's parents and my folks approve of us as a couple. We all find that we can enjoy one another's company. It's time to think about moving.

Richard is the first person to turn my eyes toward New York City. He, Darlene, and Peter visit New York; now Richard seems sour on the subject. Peter loves the jazz in Manhattan, but I mostly hear how awful the place is from Darlene. "We had to step over bums sprawled out on the sidewalk in front of St. Mark's Church!" I am strongly cautioned to stay in Chicago. New Yorkers are stuck up and they will never accept me. I will be disappointed and shamed if I move there. More and more, these challenges are piquing my interest.

Ted is making a trip to New York to do some readings. Rochelle and I plan to drive there, meet Ted, drive him home via Providence, Rhode Island, where he has stuff stored. Neil decides to drive east with us. I teach him how to handle a stick shift. We take some acid and go to Lincoln Park for the lessons. I become Neil's guru of the clutch. Things start to flash while Neil is bucking into first gear. He gets the hang of it fast enough and we skip back to Dayton Street. Naturally, I put on Hendrix; Neil, who loves to play blues guitar, has never fully appreciated Jimi before. We write some collaborations. When Neil leaves, he quickly returns beckoning me to come down to the street. At Dayton and Armitage is a big red glimmering fire truck putting out a puny car fire. Its red lights are revolving and flashing, creating throbbing bleeding gauze in the air. There seated atop the fire truck's cab is a beautiful, stately Dalmatian whose spots become portals to our dreams.

In a few days, we leave for New York. The I-80 interstate is so new that there isn't even a radio station for much of it. Neil is able to shift the gears and the driving is easy. We spend a night in Wilkes-Barre, Pennsylvania and arrive at the George Washington Bridge about noon the next day. The sun is bright on the isle of Manhattan, which glistens before us, a toothy lower jaw of a leviathan. Ted arranges for Rochelle and I to sleep on Dick and Carol Gallup's floor. We find the corner of East 4th Street and Avenue B; stagger out, feel a shower of eyeballs run over our foreign bodies. I am shocked by what I see. Garbage over-tops the cans; the sidewalk is covered in broken glass; the block resembles my image of a battle zone. We get into the Gallup apartment and find comforting books everywhere and art on the walls. Carol makes coffee and tells us how to find the F train. We walk back into the bright sun to visit the Marlborough Gallery to view a Larry Rivers show.

New York is a place of extremes. The bums are worse off and the rich are more fabulous than Chicago's. People stare at one another with wide-open appetite. This city holds a weird challenge that seems barely possible. Ted reads at the St. Mark's Poetry Project. I marvel at the dark pews, dim lights, horrible sound system, and the very lovely poetry reading. Ted also speaks at the 98 Greene Street loft series. He reads "Train Ride" for the first time to a charged audience of the poets listed in the poem. I notice one fellow that seems totally normal as he lays on a couch as a bevy of people circle him in conversation. This is Ted Greenwald and he runs this series. Ron Padgett invites us for tea. I make a wrong turn, drive down to the Battery, head up the West Side, wind through Greenwich Village back to East 13th Street. We arrive at Ron and Pat's an hour late. We stay out late and come back to East 4th Street's gallery of vicious stares from its beer-sodden denizens. Rochelle and I feel that if we can manage a sudden weekend on East 4th Street then a longer stay would not be out of the question. No one we meet says move to New York and be poets. No one wants us. We like that, something to think about while we drive Ted back to Chicago.

Ted arranges for us to pick him up at 7 a.m. at Kenward Elmslie's townhouse on Greenwich Avenue. We arrive and find him in a deep sleep on the third floor. We verbally try to wake him. He stirs and opens an eye. He closes it again and tells us in highly slurred speech that he was speeding all night and just popped a Quaalude an hour ago. Ted poignantly drawls, "But I will get up, wait!" Six hours: slow small movements, long delicate shower, exposes himself to Rochelle, speechifies, breakfasts with Kenward, hears Eric Anderson and Dave Van Ronk songs for the road. Early afternoon, we head out the Cross Bronx Expressway to Rhode Island. We all take Dexamyls and talk up the Eastern Seaboard. As we near Providence, Ted takes the wheel to guide us through the gathering dusk to his brother's house, where his boxes are stored. He doesn't have the address; he just thinks he can find it. As he ponders what direction to go, his hand hovers over the gearshift, fingers slightly waggling toward the knob before contact is made and the gear is shifted. We are going around in endless circles; Rochelle keeps saying, "Let's call them and find out," to no avail. Ted is on his turf and it will work out. An hour later, we are still gliding around curved streets that double back to nowhere. A couple of times, Ted stops and calls out to somebody, "Hey, Mack!" where is such and such street? No one knows. Rochelle reads the entire ribald novel *Two Suspicious Characters* by Katie Schneeman and Tessie Mitchell. Then when all is hopeless lost and over, we are there!

Rochelle and I have coffee with Ted's sister-in-law as he rummages through his boxes in the basement. He is looking for Alice's notebooks and valuable works of art. He brings up a beautiful signed Warhol print, *Flowers*, that is folded in half. His sister-in-law apologizes; she needed to make space. Ted politely says that it is of no import. I get the feeling this artwork looms large in his financial future. We find out how to get to Ted's youngest brother's house and visit him and his wife and new child. More coffee, we head west in the middle of the night. Take more pills. Ted takes the wheel. Shortly the car zigs sharply to the right and zags strongly to the left. Then it brakes hard. He pulls off the road to a stop, "I have just given myself the three-point driver's test and flunked." Ted talks as I drive. Ted talks near me rather than to me. He is putting a whole part of his life into perspective. It is inspiring and abstract. I feel like Dr. Wolfe does hearing my abstractions. I am flattered to be in Ted's presence, yet I am too young and naïve to retain what this Ted talk says. We stop for hamburgers at an all-night Thruway oasis. Rochelle, ripped out her skull, reads the giant plastic menu and starts exclaiming, "Oh, a grilled cheese on shit! A California shit burger! A malted shit shake!" She continues to read her amended menu in a loud voice. Ted and I are pretending not to be falling off our stools laughing. When we leave, Rochelle walks out with the menu clutched firmly under her arm.

In the predawn light, we drive through Buffalo New York and look at houses where Ted had once lived and that were no doubt a part of his personal narrative this very night. We look at houses in which Ted had written and shot speed. I secretly sob for the gray wood-frame houses and the blurry dead lake to the west. Ted points out the office of his greatest discovery in Buffalo: a doctor who writes scripts for Desoxyn. It is a small low building with a few quiet evergreens in front. Back on the empty speedway out of town at dawn, two aging narcos pull up next us at a red light. They ask us if we know where to score some grass. Ted rolls down his window and asks these guys if they have any Valium. They speed off. A few more miles down the road, Ted makes a new proposal, that we go visit Niagara Falls. Rochelle says no. Ted reminds her, "This may be the last time you'll get to see it, and it is just over there." He points abstractly into the drear landscape. Rochelle says, "No, we are going home now!" At the next gas and pee stop, Ted and I are standing at adjacent stalls. Ted laughs, "Boy, I really love Rochelle!

She knows her mind. I love her saying no to Niagara Falls!"

Back on the interstate, Rochelle and Ted fall into deep sleeps. I feel lonely, except for all the speed I am taking. I start to hallucinate drawbridges in the up position where there are none. I see sharp curves while the road stays straight. There are men standing on the edge of the road swinging their arms back and forth preparing to jump in front of my oncoming wheels. I become adept at figuring out which sights are hallucinations and which sights are real and safely drive my sleeping cargo home to sweet home Chicago.

We never decide to leave Chicago. I never feel that could even be possible. Between Rochelle and me, the rune stones had been cast and a decision made without words. As we make our new plans known to our friends, we are shocked at their reactions. It seems one cannot love Chicago and leave it. A couple of friends make it clear that if we leave, we will no longer be friends. The pressure to stay in Chicago added to our need to leave. Artistic challenge and shared adventures await us. So it finally comes down to losing a friend or two. All is not sadness in our gang; Richard and Darlene are making their wedding plans.

What is marriage? If two people live together, in one sense they grow in their mutual love; in another sense they grow more independent and somewhat poignantly unknown to the other. This is a living contract, just as a marriage is supposed to be. The question of marriage floats over Rochelle and me and we begin to see it as something outside of our relationship. A single event with no before or after; I hope for glorified electricity to see each other in perfect lucidity and to bear the electric aura that proves the moment true. Once proven, there can be no change, just the added charge of time. I unwittingly ready my proposal. Richard and Darlene marry in June, out of doors, at Illinois Beach State Park in Zion, north of Chicago. Paul Hoover officiates. He has standing in the mail-order Universal Life Church. Rochelle and I toast and dance. Darlene controls the fountain over the wedding cake. It keeps getting higher and higher. Rochelle and I dance closer, smacking our bodies across the floor.

Rochelle and I need a wedding to raise funds for the move to New York. Our prospects seem much brighter if we marry in Chicago before we go. The rabbi tells us that we do not seem like a couple that wants to get married. He gives us a book that explains sex. We peruse the sex book and bring it back. We ask Richard to write a speech for the rabbi to read. No siblings, no friends attend, just our parents. Two shy lovers, four parents, stand before the rabbi in his office, North Side Temple on Lake Shore Drive in the same room where my folks got married. The rabbi reads the seven blessings and he reads Richard's speech. We are charmed. When we place the rings, I feel an electric jolt surging through space and time to connect us. Picture-taking time, the rabbi puffs himself up; Rochelle fully turns to him and says, "Not you."

We honeymoon in White Pines Forest State Park. The cabin is nice and the restaurant is excellent. We retire to lounge in our underwear, which we don't do much. We smoke some grass as we drift off. Desperate cries of female anguish come through the open window. We are shocked and hold each other in a fearful huddle while the screams and screeches continue a short while and then stop. In the morning, we pull out and see a drive-in movie theater adjacent to the park entrance playing *Rosemary's Baby*.

My parents host a party in their Wilmette home. It is summer so there is open house with Champagne service on the porch. All my poet friends from Chicago and Iowa arrive, and so do many psychoanalysts, friends of my parents. The poets and the shrinks seem thrilled to be near one another and there is great excitement. We register for gifts so that we can cash them out. We sell the car and have a nest egg to move on. Rochelle tells me that when we get to New York, we will not be married. I understand. We are strangers on a park bench. We feel the synchronized beating of our hearts. Without the desire to move in closer, I hold Rochelle and she holds me. The proposal I keep in my pocket is now the answer on her face.

1973 - 1974

Messenger

> "There is one level at which you move between being a street person and a messenger."
> – Carl Solomon

September 5, 1973

New York – just arrived via Amtrak – Broadway Ltd. Penn. station to Hotel Chelsea, rm. 112. Temperature in the 80s / 90s, 12:15 p.m. wondering – analogous feeling – going away to college – Rochelle says, "This town sure gets dirty." No spirits – no action. The room has a pleasant green rug and a curtain with blue flowers.

Uptown, downtown – how to settle in? From the top of the Empire State Building, we look to the Upper West Side, which this day is mired in clouds of pollution. Then look to the Lower East Side, which is sweetly bathed in sunshine. The *New York Times* apartment listings direct us to a little studio on St. Mark's Place. We take it. Through the ailanthus trees, we can see the weather vane atop St. Mark's Church.

My old Chicago neighbor, Peter Scholnick, helps me find my first job in New York City. Peter Scholnick is a graphic artist and filmmaker on a career path at Gray Advertising. He knows a small commercial-art studio that needs a walking messenger. With Scholnick's good recommendation, there is no doubt about landing the job. Ralph peers over his half glasses and says, "I hear that you're interested in poetry." "Well interested is not the right word." "OK, how much would you like to make?" "I'd like to take home about $100. a week." "OK — start Monday." I leave the dark studio and jumble my feet onto East 48th Street.

At $100 a week, it only takes two weeks' work to pay the rent. Norm Heller Assoc. lies on the easy path to most of the Madison Avenue and Third Avenue advertising firms. His studio specializes in print media and has a lot of mechanicals walking in and out the door. Ralph Cardello manages the business for Norm Heller — Jewish owned, Italian run. Or Italian owned, Jewish run — the best-known Midtown business combinations. Norm's setup looks comfortable. There are six drafting boards in the front area, one of which belongs to Tommy the Retoucher. At the center of the floor is a small reception area with a secretary, and there are small offices for the bookkeeper and the boss. The type headliner and stat machines occupy a smelly black area in the far back. The studio's success depends on good renderings and speedy back and forth in the field. Even though there is not constant work, they employ three messengers. Steve is hired at the same time as I, but he is openly ambitious to get on the boards. Davey is a lanky kid from Queens who has been messengering for several months. He has a hard time making it to work every single day. His high thin cheeks are always flush from bitter winds that swirl around him. It is just a Queens' boy life of perpetual rebuff. Davey helps me plan my first deliveries and pick-ups and in general takes me under his frail wings. Clutching coffee, he whispers the hideous stories of his childhood. The man who jumps to his death in front of him makes an indelible sound as the body first hits the subway grate and then drips to the cement bottom. He cowers, left alone at night, while his mom works. Guys try to pick the locks and burglars scratch on the windows. High-strung, I conclude.

After my first day, Davey wants to buy me a beer. He walks me to a small dive on West 45th Street that turns out to be a topless bar. I am shocked that beers cost five bucks apiece. A woman is standing up on the bar slowly wiggling her breasts and leaning over to talk to an obviously regular customer. Davey and I drink and talk while the regular customer tries to teach the dancer to twirl her breasts in opposite directions. I leave Davey there and head home with a perfectly tawdry impression of a New York workday. The next day, Davey fails to show at work, in fact, he is out close to a week. He later tells me that after drinking that night, he is walking along 42nd Street and goes up to an officer of the law inquiring, "How tall do you have to be to be a cop?" He is billy-clubbed and thrown in overnight lockup. He hates going to work. He comes in less and less, pissing Ralph no end.

New York's predawn blackness rings; alarms me. I feel my way down the solid white ladder from the sleeping loft. I don't mind going to work if I have written something first. A poem before work allows me to face the IRT with a light heart. I go off with a good conscience and waste the rest of day earning money. My baby blue Olivetti is ready on top of my desk, which is a board covering an old sewing machine frame complete with a working foot treadle. I sit and pump for poetry lines while I stare through the trees of heaven to the St. Mark's weather vane. The skies stretch into polluted lavender and puce changing to a pale blue roar of traffic up the avenues. The poems need not be good; they just need to be there lounging in the Olivetti carriage all day while I toe the pavements.

In a few stops, I scramble up to the sidewalk at 51st Street, salute the spiked top of the GE building, start the walking machine. Every corner has two options. One can avoid a DON'T WALK and cross Lexington but walking down Lexington is crowded and slow. Better to wait for the WALK just to be able to cross Lexington, and zip over to Park, then walk down to 48th. Park sidewalks are broader, less peopled. There is the problem of crossing Park. Start at the first moment of WALK. Step clearly into the street; avoid the median or else become stuck behind people already standing there.

Walk around the medium because the light is short, and even if done well, one arrives across the street amid the final flashes of DON'T WALK. Norm Heller's is cheerful with coffee. There are a few mechanicals ready to go, so I grab them and turn on my heels. Walking with a large manila envelope under my arm makes me invisible.

The invisible trick is to walk about a half pace faster than the general flow and to hug the curb when passing dawdlers. The pace is keyed to the traffic sequence. The right pace gets one all the way down the block and into the green intersection. I can make green after green, but I do know there will be a red in my future. Planning dictates leaving the corner options open to allow me to turn instead of stopping. When I get into exactly the right groove, I can stay ahead of the pace, make my lights, be invisible and lost in thought. I can walk ten blocks before waking to my surroundings. I figure it is like surfing – like riding the big elevator to heaven before the wave smashes to shore. My wave breaks onto glass revolving doors.

*

Several years later as I work for Allen Ginsberg, I discover that the writer Carl Solomon, dedicatee of "Howl", is currently a working messenger. I decide to interview Carl about the job of being a messenger. I record Carl on a park bench on one of his routes; he has a manila envelope at his side:

> Carl: When I first started going down to the World Trade Center, it seemed like a fantastic new world, like going onto another planet. Enormous buildings down there – the big crowds of people running through the Trade Center and the fantastic restaurants -- shops in the Trade Center – then you get that area of Lower Manhattan, you know, John Street, Ann Street, strange stores and all kinds of establishments that go back hundreds of years. I walk across graveyards. I come across Alexander Hamilton's grave. Streets like Nassau or John for example, you watch the torrent of people coming one way – you have to go like a broken-field runner. Before I gave up smoking, I would bang into people and hit people with the cigarettes; now that I have given up cigarettes it is considerably easier, much less friction with other people.

> Bob: Are you walking ahead of the traffic or with the traffic?

> Carl: Against the traffic – there's one turn [around] there, like 140 Broadway is a big building, which is the front of One Chase Plaza. So when you're going down around closing time around five o'clock, they come like a horde of cattle. They're coming at great speed because most of 'em are practically running, cause they just got off work, and they're going this way and you're going the other way so you have to find your path very carefully and walk very defensively. And then there are days

when you're walking and there are storms in midsummer when there is a thunder and lightning storm – when the rain is coming down hard while you decide what to do. You can either wait under something until it stops or I play games – I play imaginative games with myself, little ego games, and I decided well I am going to go out – I don't give a damn about the consequences – I am going to go out and walk through the rainstorm and get drenched and it'll dry on me – so I did that – and I got a little applause, which pleased me, from the people I was serving. "Gee, you came through the rain!" they make kind of a fuss over me.

*

The object is to hand over the package and to hand it over to the right person or make sure it lands on the right desk. Only one person is in the way: the receptionist. When the elevator doors slide back, I get into the middle of the bunch of folk going past the receptionist. If I am alone emerging onto the floor, I just stride past the receptionist. She might call me back, "Who are you looking for?" They might say, "Just leave it here, I'll see that he gets it." Bullshit! They might let you stand there with the boards under your arm. They might call the guy and he will be slow to come out and be put out with me, having to come forward. The receptionists were mostly temps and don't know who is who anyway. I try to get into the office pool. Anybody there can point the mark out to me. It is better to find the marks and slide the package under their noses with great aplomb. They look up and smile and Norm Heller Assoc. is tops again. A lot I care. I care for me. Most of the time I really do know where the art director hangs out and I wave to the receptionist saying, "I know where he is." The old messengers with ripped, snotty sleeves, floppy hats, cold fingers, red noses wait every time. They totter there before the pristine college girls. I am 23 and White – I am allowed to swim in the office pool.

The regular customers want me to wait while they look over the mechanical. Often I carry it right back to the studio for modifications. The ones who trust me give me the changes verbally without calling Ralph. I come out after conversing with the gods and find a bunch of miserable old men waiting as the receptionist examines her nails. The elevator bongs open and I occupy the rear corner so my boards can go flat against the wall.

Fast walking – dark windows on Mad – bright windows on Park – people packing Fifth – all plazas on Sixth, old messengers huddle in doorways trying to get their bearing out of the wind – speedy bike messengers fly in and out of traffic with their heavy chains draped across their chests. Bikes are insane – feet are sane! Two rules: 1. Whenever feasible, walk though Rockefeller Center and stop to watch the skaters. 2. If possible, ride the Burlington House Mill conveyor belt for a psychedelic display of threads and weaves which lets me out en route that much closer.

When in the street, one pays attention to vehicles. They want to chase you out of the crosswalk, and you do not want to degrade yourself by running out of their impending doom. I discover a slow-fast shuffle, which prevents accidents. As a taxi or truck bears down, I take short quick steps that simulate hurrying, yet in reality only speed me up a little. Likewise, the vehicle slows down without braking, so no one gets hit or gives in to the other. Often, just one or two fake shuffles appeases a driver who will fake slow early.

While pacing up an avenue, I hear all the people talking to themselves: crazy patchwork of self-accusations, home arguments, silly ditties, profound strings of foul swearing. I am absorbed into the Midtown fabric. I sing as I storm through its weave. I think poetry. I race cars. Alone in an express elevator to the fiftieth floor what else to do but jump up and down to feel the floor rise to meet your feet, no falling except that thin cable and if it snaps – what the hell!

*

Bob: What about elevators? How do you feel about elevators? When you're shooting up fifty floors nonstop?

Carl: Or to the 102nd floor of the World Trade Center! Well in the beginning I actually did things like say my prayers when I got into 'em. I thought this would be a good place to start praying, and I also got the feeling like participating in some kind of Hollywood movie like *Stairway to Heaven*. I look at the other people there and say to myself, "Well we're going up God knows where but we're all in this together."

Bob: Like figuring if you had to spend the next five years with these people.

Carl: Like Sartre's *No Exit*.

Bob: Does it do anything to you? I mean obviously you spend a good part of your day going up and down in elevators.
Carl: Now in this day of robotics I tend to psychoanalyze each elevator.

Bob: How do you do that?

Carl: Well some elevators have certain peculiarities, will stop at a certain time, be temperamental at certain times, you have to realize that you are living in the day and age of robotics and try to get elevators that are more docile, that are more compliant, better adjusted elevators you know – you don't want the neurotic elevators.

Bob: That whip up and stop short.

Carl: Yeah, elevators are like people.

Bob: Are you ever alone in the elevators?

Carl: Sometimes, but I keep my cool – I think to myself, "Where are the emergency buttons?" I myself am very safety conscious and think to myself, "Do I know what to do in an emergency?"

Bob: I used to jump up while expressing up, and the elevator would meet me half-way down. It was frightening.

Carl: Well yeah, we all go through that.

*

Ralph Cardello commutes from Ozone Park. He is always the first one in. He is fair-minded. He is swarthy skinned, cheerful; he knows the whole business. He appreciates me because I am fast. Once I am given the dimensions for a three-dimensional box, a ruler, and money. I have to search stores for these dimensions for a product mock-up. I am measuring boxes; the manager of the Gristedes comes up and demands, what I am doing. When I tell him, he swears to the skies about advertising agencies. I finally find a box of granola that will become the first box of Stove Top Stuffing! I get to take the unwanted granola home. As long as I do my tasks well, Ralph doesn't mind reading. I am reading a lot of Kerouac and thinking a lot about Ozone Park. I like to redesign paperback book covers. I sit behind an empty drafting table reading a paperback with a green blotter paper cover and fierce Sgt. Fury blazing machine guns. Ralph snatches it out of my hands and flips to the title page, expecting to find something salacious; he finds Homer's the *Iliad*. Ralph hands the book back and says, "You won't work here long."

Tommy the Retoucher is freelance. He is a busy, wisecracking, Italian. Most every day, I pick up the raw photographs from Bloomingdales. The ladies in underwear look so sensual before Tommy airbrushes out pubic hairs, diminishes fleshy navels, and obliterates slight rolls of skin and wrinkles, all the while adding the proper shadows. Tommy and Ralph are pals and always lunch together.

Davey and I are the only messengers. Steve starts with me but now is always on the boards. Davey becomes less and less reliable. Norm doesn't know what to do so he gives Davey a big Christmas bonus, which encourages Davey never to come back. "I tried," Norm sighs. "Dumb kid!" Ralph says.

Often Ralph hands me taxi money. That stays money in my pocket because I learn how to loop Midtown on the subways. Taxi fares are my only real perk. The subways are usually quicker than Midtown auto traffic. A taxi will always stop for a messenger. Messengers tip well with company money.

Walking catches up to my feet. The first month they are just sore then they start to swell each night. When I get home, I lie down and put my feet up on the wall. After fifteen minutes of draining, they feel normal again. I jump into the tub in the kitchen while Rochelle fixes a supper around me. Sometimes a cup of black coffee balanced on the edge of the tub gets knocked in; I soak in the blissful dark waters.

A messenger is pure poetry. They deliver the goods. Screw what they are, they're not in control, but the delivery is really something. I write a poem about it.

MESSENGER

midtown blue & high up
   things to do
      or not so proud
     find the electric
     touch

         Watusi on 53rd street
          gold reflections melt
         the tribe is of sin

only that
    the eagle has landed
    a girl with green eyes
  pictures upon pictures of her kissing
        and she has refused all of them

  I have a funny feeling the background is white
  though looks so blue
        like glass

  take two options on one corner
cab air
    up twenty floors
       how lovely she is!

  here is your package

I get to know my routes well; I also get to know the art directors I am constantly waiting on. They are young and nervous and casual. Eventually they would ask me a personal question, to which I would reply that I write poetry. Their looks kill me; the look of romantic jealousy combined with the personal sense of loss over the abandonment of their own artistic ambitions. The art director is much worse off than I. I have to deliver bits and pieces of the golden calf but my mind is on the Ten Commandments. For them to stop milking the golden cow, which gives the BMWs, the ski weekends, the shrinks, the gold collections, would mean ripping the rings out of their noses. I stand in a fiftieth-floor office in the GM building looking over the beautiful and vast view of Central Park. It all seems to belong to the art director; but I get to keep the park forever. All he gets is the package.

Messengers don't talk to one another. They silently count each other in elevators, in lobbies, at corners, in coffee shops, on the curb. Messengers just think about their feet. They look down and fade into corners. It's a loner art. They walk in their own world, where people's stares pass through them like endless doses of microwaves. They shrivel up and disappear into the glare of the avenues. Yet messengers are individuals culled out of the offices and cast into the street pool. There is intelligence under the flesh gained from rubbing knuckles with the multitude. They turn the corner; they shuffle down an eternal number of streets knowing they will tread these streets again for a lifetime more. They are all hugging the curb, defensively walking against the flow of feet. Stepping between the sneers, they leave multitudes behind in their wake. No wonder they are proud of their skills of rationality, considering the complex social position and minimum wage.

*

Carl: I get silly sometimes. When I really deteriorate, I get silly and talk like a baby or make up stupid rhymes or absurd shocking things and repeat them, and sometimes in some of the games I go through I think of myself as being a childhood hero like Charlemagne at the Battle of Roncevaux Pass, you know, or I think I'm Orlando Furioso, or think I'm fighting the Huron in the American Indian Wars. I think I'm some sort of hero to buoy myself up.

Bob: Are you a messenger in the fantasy?

Carl: Right. I'm helping the American forces aid the British in the French and Indian Wars – it's very important! It's very important to get there. I actually do these things and its sort of embarrassing to mention it – actually, I'm crazy as a bed bug, but I don't lose the link to reality so that a cop has to come up and ask, "Are you fighting the French and Indian Wars now?" I'm not crazy, though some messengers are. And this mixes up my politics because my politics may be against many aspects of American foreign policy but my fantasy is very pro-American. Fantasy and patriotism get mingled.

Bob: There is nobility here. It is a noble service you perform.

Carl: Well, I have to do it; otherwise, I wouldn't be able to do it. I used to be told that I was an extraordinary messenger.

*

The stated Midtown rule is: Never go into an elevator alone with a Black man. I am alone delivering a mechanical to a small studio in the furthest East 50s, a quiet block with low buildings and few people. As I wait in the lobby for the poky elevator, a well-dressed Black man enters the lobby. The fear wells up in me. I tell myself that I can't subscribe to racist dictums and look the guy over. He is much better dressed than me, and besides, I am carrying a large manila envelope – the badge of a poor messenger. He asks me for the time. I pull up my sleeve to glance at my cheap Timex and tell him. We both get into the elevator. I push three and he pushes four. Between the second and third floors, he turns to me and asks if I have a quarter. "Huh?" I am surprised as he blocks me into the corner with his shoulder. I can't see his face anymore but I can see his hand slip into his pocket and pull out a steak knife. He doesn't put it to my throat. He just displays it like showing an ID card. I am thankful that for once I have five dollars on me. "Give me your money or I'll stick you," he informs me. I reach for my wallet saying, "OK you got it, no problem, do me a favor, just leave the wallet on the floor." I hand him the wallet and get off on the wrong floor – the one he pushed. He takes the elevator down. I wait for the elevator to come back while slowly slipping into shock. The doors open and my wallet is on the floor. The studio reimburses my fiver and the bookkeeper tells me to double the amount stolen if I file a police report – its deductible. I don't file. I am a nervous wreck the rest of day; this is Rochelle's 22nd birthday.

My first New York spring is dawning. Sweet ocean breezes jump onto the city subtly stripping clothes off the walkers on the avenues. Shortly before I quit, I get a raise. Norm says it is because I am fast. I realize that I made a mistake. I have gotten too fast. I am burning up the Midtown blocks with speed, and the wind bends back my ears. The exhilaration of the day's mad pace doesn't leave me at night. Sleep comes harder. My mind roars along littered streets, jumps up and down in elevators, dodges bucking taxis. I take longer breaks overlooking the skaters in Rockefeller Center. The ringers who skate there every day and do simple worn-out figures look shabby; the visitors who flop down and giggle seem stupid. I dart into St. Patrick's Cathedral and dash out. I am looking for a way out. I am no longer just a new fish. The street pace is too rich a soup to swim in full throttle. The more it gets to be spring, the more I want to stop. I apply for a training session to teach poetry in New York City public schools and tender my resignation to Ralph. He smiles. I suggest that I might need the job back, but Ralph says, "You'll never be a messenger again."

It is dawn. The cock on the weathervane always points west towards Chicago. But the spring gusts blow everything about. Rochelle and I get a cheaper apartment further east. Rochelle picks up some work in a gallery. My feet are no longer sore. I feel disarranged, but my head is tethered to the non-business of poetry. I look up from the pale blue Olivetti and gaze into the hard blue Midtown sky. The weathercock on St. Mark's steeple points to me and the sea beyond.

Photo by Morris Rosenthal 437 East 12th Street around 1976.

1975 – 1977

Fifth Avenue Overhead

I

Deciding to quit the cleaning business is difficult. It in effect *spoils* me: I am my own boss I work when I want to and not work if I don't feel up to it I have regular customers, I have no need for advertising. I no longer have to take those awful one-time-only massive cleanups. I am getting more work than I care to handle and start to refer customers to other cleaners. Obviously, the next step is to start my own referral service. Saving myself for only the most preferred customers, I would enlist others to handle the bulk of the jobs. But this is a step that I am not prepared to take. Taking responsibility for other people's work and being responsible for their fair treatment would be a giant headache. I do not enlarge my cleaning business; I do become weary of the work. My book about my experiences cleaning people's home is about to come out. It seems impossible to clean after that, except to be chic. I am about to finish graduate school so I decide to quit the cleaning business at the same time.

Looming before me is the production of *Bicentennial Suicide*. Bob Holman and I have written two plays together. We produce one of them on stage and the other is performed live on WBAI. This new one is to be the blockbuster of our collaborations; it is set to open at the Soho Rep on July 4, 1976. We decide to work on it separately because Bob is off to trek in Africa and I am staying in the city to finish up at CCNY. I do quit cleaning in the spring to throw myself fully into writing *Bicentennial Suicide.* The physicality of house cleaning for several years barely prepares me for the Herculean task of writing, producing, and performing in *BiSi.*

The importance of *BiSi* to this essay, it being centered on working and not theater, is that it wrecks my health. I am sure that this will sound corny, but I feel that this production is the high point of my official youth. I am 27 years old. My parents always assure me that youth is about *acting out*, which they feel is rarely useful or profitable. That is, if you can criticize youth for being childish, I can't. The month that Bob and I spend mounting the play is pure work. We rehearse the cast (including ourselves) six days a week. Spend every available moment organizing costumes, theater sets, tech people; composing new parts; publishing a book simultaneously to the event.

The play itself is complicated, and the social history of the cast is even more so. I must add that any words about *backstage* would be disquieting because all of our sins, regrets, pleasures, and enmities become transformed *on the stage*. The off-stage always

51

leads to nowhere in the theater and is better left undefiled. The exercises of rehearsal stretch my body, which tightened up from cleaning. The yoga of theater is a painful procedure but also a nice way to descend from the heights of hard labor.

During the composition of *BiSi*, I hit upon a structure of alternating *hard* and *soft* sections. Hard sections are poetically formal and push the storyline of the love affair between Uncle Sam and Columbia, Gem of the Ocean, and the soft sections are prosy and digressive, allowing many new characters and access points to the themes of the play. It is the essence of American literature to mix nonfiction (hard) and fiction (soft) together.

By the time opening night rolls around, I am suffering from a throat infection that turns my voice to gravel, makes me sweat profusely, and causes rippling urges to cough while on stage. I gargle with salt water and expectorate globs of phlegm and drink cough syrup at each offstage exit. My health slowly returns during the run of the play. I had indulged myself with a cigarette habit. I quit it now. I still have a low tolerance for tobacco smoke. I want to go on and on about the wasting of my health. I love the subject! The golden joys on the climb back to health inspire deep and undisturbed poetic reveries. After *Bicentennial Suicide* closes, Rochelle and I leave town to recoup our strength, and hopefully we will want to see our best friends again.

II

We come back to the city in the fall. My August birthday horoscope for the year predicts that my financial picture will improve after the New Year. This is good, as I have no intention of looking for employment. I do not want to use my new M.A. to find work. I don't want to teach; I feel this would deprive me of necessary experiences that will give me something to teach when I am older. Rochelle is the secretary at the Poetry Project and our apartment costs only $125 a month. I don't feel compelled to jump into the job market. I lazily put the word out that I am looking for work. I feel secure that this passive method will succeed. I don't actively search work-wanted ads or go on interviews. I still receive many cleaning requests, which I dutifully turn down. I am eager to see what the future brings and taking an occasional cleaning job will cause me delays. I want to stay home and write. Our building, alas, is not being given any heat or hot water, so I am forced to get out of the house to seek warmth and a shower at friends' apartments.

January 2, 1977, is a lucky day. There is hot water, and I take a bath. Lucky because I think to bring the phone near the tub in case it rings; it does. It's Michael Andre, whom I think I have met but know I have corresponded with. He says he heard that I might be able to help him out. Michael goes on to explain things, which clouds up what it is he wants of me. I gather he needs general help fixing up his loft. Maybe Michael just needs moral encouragement, common sense, but I figure it will be pretty physical too. The job seems less menial than cleaning and comes with remuneration; I accept. Unfortunately, I do have to step out of the tub in the kitchen to go dripping into the living room to write down Andre's address and phone number.

Andre has a block-long loft on the short block below Canal on Lispenard Street, just off Broadway. He is living with Erika Rothenberg; they are an item. She works as an art director at an advertising agency, and Michael is supposed to *do* home improvements. The loft has a spacious open area on the Canal Street side that is separated from the Lispenard side by a Plexiglas wall with a door cut out of it. The door itself is most interesting. Like a hatch in a submarine, one has to step through it. The ovoid opening is about one cubit off the floor. With this arrangement, one can seal half of the loft from the other. The Lispenard end has Erika's sofa, coffee table, a vintage office desk, an open kitchen and a small bedroom.

Michael's projects are to repair and paint the ceiling, build shelves, rewire light fixtures, and remove a protruding kitchen counter to open up the space. The repair to the ceiling is the daunting chore that makes him call me to help. The ceiling is pockmarked with small holes that once held sweatshop machinery. Michael can't face the tedious chore of filling all these tiny holes with putty.

Rochelle and I have our eyes open for a good loft living situation; this job seems like an opportunity to get better acquainted with what it is like, even if the work is menial and unskilled. I work for Michael once a week and spend many weeks on a ladder filling in those holes in the tin ceiling.

Michael is always a good host; he puts out a nice lunch and we talk literary gossip. He is interested in *Cleaning Up New York*, my manual on cleaning houses. I tell him I will not give him a copy until I am out of his employ. I am sensitive to my descriptions of pilfering drugs from my customers. He will think that I am searching for his secret spots, but ironically I am not looking. I actually like filling in those holes. The illusion of an unending chore is that it is not endless. When I work, I am calmed by the knowledge that the task is finite. I spend a day in the bedroom closet, installing shelves for linens; bend and twist and crouch to work there. I am crumpled and mystified at how the shelving installs without screws. Needless to say, Michael and I do not work together except for the day we rip out the offensive kitchen counter. Michael is not eager to do it, but I agree with Erika that the space will be much better with the counter out of the way. I'm eager to see some radical change here. Ripping the cabinets off the floor and off the wall has a couple exciting moments, but the hardest work is to get rid of them. We carry it down to Canal Street and walk with it. Two guys walking cross Canal with a large counter between them are the least visible of all folks, shopping, hawking, going to school, contemplating crimes. We walk a few blocks up and leave it against the side of a building; walk away without a word, feeling cool as if we had just robbed the post office.

Bob Holman is hustling a series of jobs; he calls them scams. One of them is a seat belt survey and inspection job. This involves going to an assigned street corner and looking down into cars stopped at a red light to see if the driver is wearing the seat belt. This is a scam because Bob can get the job done in half the allotted time. In his mind, he has doubled his salary. Bob's other scam is working at an employment agency where he is alone in an office and can leave early and sign out late. Bob stalks me out in my unemployed slough.

"Bob here!" He has a job running a small offset printing press – AB Dick 360 – at a small Wall Street financial firm – First Boston Co. Bob is under the impression that since I can run the mimeo machine at the St. Mark's Poetry Project . . . I tell Bob that I am not so sure that I am qualified for this press. Bob says he will check out the amount of skill required and get back to me. I have no idea who Bob talks to, but he calls back; says. "If you can run a mimeo machine, you can run this machine." He adds that the firm is small and not busy, so there will be little pressure at first.

I take the subway downtown and decide to have lunch to fortify myself for the job interview. This is my first time confronting the financial district on a weekday. I have walked here before on a Sunday, when the canyons are as austere as Monument Valley, Arizona. Now I am caught in a raging stream of people. Yes, I have ebbed and flowed with Midtown traffic, but Wall Street has a frantic distraction that takes time to adjust to. I turn onto Maiden Lane and squeeze into a Walgreen's lunch counter. All of a sudden I feel like a total hick. All of the counter seats are filled, hungry patrons pace back and forth waiting for a stool to be vacated. I notice a seat but don't see the occupant leave it. I foolishly ask the guy next to it if it is taken. He turns to me staring blankly, then returns to his food. Uneasily, I sit down and glance at the menu. A waitress furiously approaches and demands my order. "I'd like a BLT and a milk shake, please." "Order by numbers!" she barks back. Then I notice all the menu items have numbers affixed to them. I search again for my order but she interrupts, "A BLT is a 97 and the milk shake is a 46." She notes this in her pad and zips off. Within a few minutes, my 97 and 46 appear before me; the sandwich tastes like cardboard with tomato juice and bit of crunch, the milk is thin. I eat as fast as humanly possible, pay, and disappear.

I feel better now; the job interview can be no worse than the lunch. I quickly walk to Exchange Place and find First Boston Co.; as I walk into the lobby, I notice that this company occupies most of the building. I find the main desk and tell them why I am here. The young woman looks hard at me with a puzzled expression and sends me to the mailroom two floors down. This room is the entire floor. Off to the side is a glassed-in section with four large printing presses; three of them are feverishly spitting out paper, and one is idle. I get the feeling this is not going to work out as I approach the print shop supervisor. He is a burly middle-aged Black man; he regards me coldly. Asks what experience I have. I explain that I have no experience but was told none was necessary. If I could run a mimeograph machine, . . . He is dubious and so am I; I am about to turn to leave when he says that he will give me a test. Two minutes on the machine to see what I can do. Reluctantly and somewhat cavalierly, I agree. He calls over to George, the only White guy down there, to set me up on the machine. The young men at the machines jerk their heads up to notice me; then rivet their attention back on their machines. George shows me where the smocks are. I pick one up and try to figure out how to put it on when he says, "You can use one of those," pointing a pile of a different-colored smock. I start to sense the deep hierarchy of race and age. I approach the machine and realize I have no idea how to run it. The supervisor comes over and hands me a stencil and tell me to start. I manage to get the stencil on and start the machine rolling because there is a big switch labeled ON/OFF. The machine is loaded with paper; the next task is to get the paper moving over the drum. George whispers, "Air, use your air." I grasp a lever marked AIR; lo and behold, a thin tube blows under the paper and it starts to travel through the machine. I am looking over the controls; I know the next task is inking the drum. George is about to offer another hint when the supervisor yells over not to help. I fail to ink the machine. Test over. "Enough" the supervisor says and returns to his desk. I shut the machine down, take off the smock and walk out trying not to look behind me. I go back to the supervisor and say, "I am not trying to cause you any trouble; I am just looking for a job and I have to follow every lead." he looks up at me slightly gloating, 'I understand." I leave the mailroom and empty out back to the street. I am shaking with anger. I realize that all of that was unnecessary. I feel degraded and humiliated; it is the supervisor's psychodrama. I find a phone booth and call Bob to complain. He is genuinely surprised. I advise Bob that this place will only hire African Americans. I don't think I have ever so clearly been on the other end of the White stick. The small dose of rage I get does not discriminate. Bob tells me later his boss says, "Yeah, they never hire Whites there."

While less eager than before to look for work, a cash crisis is brewing in my household. A quart of beer is now a thrill we can ill afford. Bob no longer works at the employment agency because he has been promoted to district coordinator for the seat belt survey job. He needs a couple new survey takers and asks me if I am game. As unappealing as standing out all day in the March cold is, I gratefully accept. Bob gives me an orientation looking into cars parked in SoHo. On an intake chart, we record: the license plate number, the model type, the color, the type of seat belt on board (lap or shoulder/lap), the age and gender of the driver. There seems like a lot to take note of, but it is not hard to do with parked cars with no drivers. My first assignment is Main Street, Flushing, Queens. I am glad that my first spot will be in a middleclass neighborhood. I put on long underwear, grab my clipboard and ID badge; catch the Flushing line to Main Street. Alone on the windswept expanse of thoroughfare, I am waiting for the red light. A car stops and I step off the curb and commence to write down its license plate number. The driver notices me and starts to pull away. I walk forward to look in the front window. I have to look down into the driver's lap to note if the belts are being used. The driver freaks and speeds away. I remember Bob saying that one has to be "quick, official, and fearless." "Keep in mind you are screwing the company by doing the work in half the time!" It gives me enough courage to keep trying. Whenever the lights turn green, I gratefully return to the sidewalk to hop around to stay warm. I try to grab the license number on the first car as it comes to a stop. But I am dysgraphic and can't get them correctly onto the form. People maneuver their cars to prevent me from finishing my entry. After fifteen minutes, I only have a couple of entries. I will need more than the allotted time to provide the required number of entries. I hate every second.

A woman pulls over after I record her; she demands to know what I am doing. "Seatbelt survey, federal government." She gives me a disgusted look. People just don't trust the government. My ability to take down the license numbers disappears; the situation is impossible. I call Bob and try to explain but I have only one quarter. I give him the number (I think) to call me back. He never does. I pace out in the cold until my feet start to walk to the subway. I go straight to Holman's, just in time for lunch: "When I called back and got a Chinese laundry, I knew you had split." The irony of it all is that I always wear a seat belt when I drive. I consider it an act of good luck. When the study is released the following year, it reports what we all know, that practically no one wears seat belts.

III

A big green lizard gazes down Fifth Avenue. One hundred feet long and thirty feet high, his vermillion tail hangs off the side of a three-story brick edifice at the corner of 13th Street and Fifth Avenue. His fire engine-red tongue lustily gobbles up air and his light-bulb eyes send rays of red light through the black void to a lone star wheeling over the avenue. Beneath this garish lizard is a rather stately, venerable building with two large bay windows. The overall squat shape of the building is more reminiscent of a bank than the trendy, tasteless honkytonk it claims to be.

My friend Alfred Milanese works as a bartender there. He tells me they are looking for a part-time bookkeeper. I am interested. Nothing happens, then out of the blue Alfred calls me from the bar and tells me to come in for an interview. I walk west along St. Mark's Church's back fence to the back of Grace Church at 4th Avenue, then zigzag over to Fifth. I am daydreaming of Frank O'Hara living across from Grace with Joe LeSueur. Turn uptown into bright downtown traffic to search for the address; I look for a bar and miss it. I feel crazy as I pace from 10th Street to 14th and back. "Where is it?" I cross to the west side of the Avenue at 13th and look back across. There it is! A huge red banner proclaims TOO MUCH IS NOT ENOUGH and a flagpole flies a Lone Star Cafe pennant.

As I walk back across the avenue I notice a Texas State flag pinned up over the revolving door. Is this some kind of club, like the Boy Scouts? Alfred had told me it is a country and western nightclub. I enjoyed live country and western music in Chicago; listened to Loretta Lynn and Conway Twitty, Tammy Wynette, Merle Haggard, Roy Acuff, Jimmie Rodgers, Bob Wills, Lynn Anderson. Flexing my forearms, I push through the revolving door of what many New Yorkers remember as once being a Schrafft's ice-cream parlor. The interior's brown wood bar and darkly-stained booths remind other New Yorkers that this space also does time as a Brew Burger. Alfred is behind the bar. I go in and sit down.

Alfred pours me a coke and calls down to the office in the basement. He tells me about the job situation: Mort Cooperman and Thomas Keane are the owners; Tony Brauer is the manager. The job entails answering the phone, taking messages, and doing light bookkeeping. Tony doesn't have enough time to do it. I am learning my place as I wait a long time to be called to the basement office. Alfred leads me down and introduces me to the owners. Leaning back in a swivel chair behind a commanding desk is the handsome Thomas Keane. Standing hunched over in the corner is an older, less formal man; Mort Cooperman has glasses, mustache, and shoe-polish brown hair. Mr. Cooperman closes the door and locks it. Suddenly all the air in the room is used up. Mr. Keane says that he doesn't know what Alfred has told me and outlines the same job but this time it is the owners that don't have time to answer the phone. He asks me if I know anything about country and western music. I lie and say I grew up with it and mention I once heard Claude King play in Chicago. King is pretty obscure, and they have never heard of him. They ask me about my education, and I half-heartedly mention my M.A. in writing. "We won't hold that against you," Thomas jokes. Mort asks if I have had any accounting courses or previous experience. Without hesitation, I tell them no. Mort turns his head away. I figure interview over and get up to leave. Thomas asks me to start Monday; I sit down again. One to five in the afternoon weekdays at $3.50 an hour. *Not enough* puts beer back on the table.

The standby quart of Ballantine Ale? No, I buy a good bottle of bourbon in anticipation of some future dollars of income, no matter how slight. Looking up is always a new direction. I go to Hudson's Army-Navy store on Third Avenue to buy a new pair of blue genes. I ignore Thoreau's warning to avoid ventures that require new clothes but don't provide intellectual growth or spiritual change. Buying new clothes to me is a way to celebrate not the new employment but rather the surcease of the search itself. The job search is deep within oneself; finding work is discovering an absolute truth. The body of knowledge acquires the job and bends it to one's vision. My scam is to mutate existence into a wisdom practice. It is not the job's task to alter my consciousness. It is only mine. Any job will equally delight. I cancel a poetry reading in Chicago scheduled for the next week. I pull up my Western jeans with a slight boot cut flair; get back into the workforce, open to discovering something new about myself.

At first Keane and Cooperman are too busy to see me. I sit at the bar. Alfred starts me answering the phone; there are two lines and a hold button. I don't yet know the upcoming acts or the names of the wait-staff. The phone rings; I don't know how to transfer the call; I stammer. Alfred testily grabs the phone and fields the call. He is annoyed that he has to teach me how to use the phones. This is not within his scope of work. I do learn the phones, and bosses in the basement seem surprised to hear my voice. Tony Brauer saunters through the revolving door. He has blond hair and a blond mustache and he is just short enough that I know he and Rochelle would like each other. I do nothing for two hours except answer the phones and get stared at by the waiters. At 3 p.m. Thomas comes up and tells me to leave. The next day is the same; I am sent home early. This time I look disgruntled about it and Thomas promises to get me started the next day, which he does.

I add taxes and gratuities to a large bill from a record company party. I take messages for Mort, but all my directions come from Thomas. The main thrust of my job is to master the phones. I learn to be completely noncommittal about a person's presence in the nightclub until I get the name and purpose of the caller. Then I say, "I will try to find him." Punch HOLD while eyeballing Mort or Thomas across the desk. "I am sorry, he doesn't seem to be here. May I take a message?" I have to pester Mort to give me verbal descriptions of the acts. Mort does all the bookings; Thomas keeps the books. I don't have much to do. I am supposed to be an office worker, but much of the time I am ordered out and the door is locked behind me. It becomes a joke to everyone else when I trudge up the stairs with some papers to work on. "Locked out again!" Tony snickers.

Not many people lunch in the restaurant. I figure it is because they are so new. I don't know how to get food out of the kitchen yet, but it smells good. I assume they make their money at night when the bands play. The service staff has to wear blue jeans and white shirts. Even in his proletarian uniform, Alfred is a suave bartender. Not only does he pour drinks with a proper air of concentration, but he also knows how to mix drinks to exact standards. A great-tasting drink can make all the difference to one's enjoyment in a shakedown nightclub like the Lone Star. There is a cover and a one-drink minimum. Alfred is the lord of the bar. He is like the head of an octopus connected to all aspects of the business. He cannot be taken advantage of by management. When he is busy, he is a prick.

Christian is the head cook—tall with short red hair, he has an effusive personality. During my first week Christian tells me that if anyone calls asking for him by name I should say, "He doesn't work here anymore." Or "He committed suicide!" But if anyone calls for Roast Beef, put him right through. If one works in a restaurant, it is vital to stay on the cook's good side. Christian is an inventive cook. He makes a fine chili, which is the hallmark of the Lone Star menu. He also makes Dolly's Legs, named after Dolly Parton, chicken legs stuffed with spiced chopped-chicken liver. Almost tempting. The mainstays of the kitchen are all types of hamburgers. I know because I tally each day's checks and track the menu items' sales. Salads are popular, but nothing sells in enough quantities to suggest a successful restaurant.

Tony is a good manager. He is not stuck up and not above helping out a beleaguered waitress, porter, cook, or bartender. Tony comes out of a music venue background and knows how to create a warm atmosphere in a room. I am not being given enough work and don't want to lose hours. I ask Tony if he has any work for me. Through Tony, I learn how the Lone Star really works. We often work together in the little office downstairs and do real work: ordering, employee schedules, payroll. I see money in and money out, and it does not add up to profitable.

The Lone Star starts out lucky. Several employees have double skills. John, a waiter, is better at building tables than serving them. He fixes the doors and counters; serves as in-house graphic designer. Eddie, a cook with a full beard, is a self-taught electrician. He provides additional telephones beyond Ma Bell's knowledge. There is a large supply of pretty waitresses drawn from the New York University community. I get to know Nancy, an experienced waitress who works the main floor tables. She will out-last any of the other waitresses with her intense way of looking into one. The whole staff is friendly and talented. I post each week's work schedule; my name is not on it. I am not on the service staff. I wonder what I will do if the service crew starts to get organized into a union.

I am a junior exec, and as one of the bosses, I do get to know my bosses. Thomas recently managed a Barnes & Noble bookstore and before that worked at Bloomingdales. I notice threatening letters from Bloomingdales. He is even-tempered and secretive; he gets mad swiftly and severely, but then he is over it quickly. Thomas overhears me talking about poetry. He asks what kind of poetry I write. I offer some personal art theory about word selections that assemble machines. He shifts his tack and asks who my favorite poets are. "O'Hara, Creeley, Berrigan, Corso, Whalen." He considers this a second and supposes that they have done some good work. He asks me who that poet is who everyone likes but no one can understand. "John Ashbery?" "Yeah." Thomas sighs, sadly shaking his head. "Who is your favorite poet?" I ask. "Dante."

Thomas keeps having me do meaningless charts. I often run errands and occasionally type letters. I still have time to look busy and cultivate my friendships in the kitchen or gossip at the bar. A few favors here and there are rewarded with after-work hamburgers, salads, chili, drinks. The jukebox plays country and western all afternoon. If patrons don't feed it, the bar gives me a couple of bucks to program it. There is a hideous number about a sexualized fling called "Afternoon Delight" that I grow to love. I am the most essential useless person around; I do everything but nothing meaningful.

Mort Cooperman comes out of advertising. He gets turned on by country music and decides to risk everything on it. The Lone Star is Mort's brainchild. He, more than anyone else, sets the tone for the nightclub. He exudes New York's frantic energy in untold directions but leans back in utter stillness with a serene smile to drink in a country tune performed in his Fifth Avenue showcase. In time, Mort begins to rely on me for some of his chores. He would throw together sloppy mechanicals for advertising, which I take to the printers to reproduce as postcards. I have to hound him for copy to get these mechanicals done in time for advertising and listing deadlines. Mort is distracted and irrational; he lets off steam in uncoordinated small jerks and bursts. He honestly loves current Country and Western but has no interest in its origins or originators. I ask him what he thinks of Hank Snow. "I hate him!" His formula is to offer Country talent a classy New York venue but pay very little in fees. Often record companies foot the bill to bring high-quality talent to appear before the print and radio media at sponsored parties. The Lone Star wants to be the place for country in New York. WHN AM radio is all-country and topping the ratings. The Lone Star and WHN trade drinks and food for executives in exchange for free on-air advertising. There are even live broadcasts from the Lone Star.

Texas is the Lone Star State, and New York is loaded with wealthy Texans. The Lone Star Cafe wants to be headquarters for these Texans in New York. The bar astutely follows the progressive musicians of Austin: Asleep At The Wheel, Greezy Wheels, Willie Nelson, Waylon Jennings. The club maintains high prices to maintain a feeling of exclusivity to patrons. There are cheaper seats in the balcony for students. *The Austin Chronicle* runs a feature on the Lone Star with a big picture in its sunday supplement. The article is highly favorable but the picture reveals that the Texas flag over the door is hung upside-down; "Mexico! We Surrender!" is our message. Dozens of indignant letters arrive and the flag is righted.

There is a third partner at the Lone Star. He was Mort's boss in advertising and is still at the agency; he is heavily invested in the club. He comes down most evenings after work. Bill McGivney is tall and thin, his complexion is white as toilet paper. His white hair makes him look like an animate X-ray. There is a host of lesser investors who come in evenings; they are Mort's friends. The Lone Star is top-heavy with investors, partners, managers, staff. The rent is astronomical; Con Ed steam bills are staggering year-round. I add it up and we come out deeply in the red each month. Mort tells me that a deficit is to be expected until the place "takes off!"

I stay late at the Lone Star only a few times. It is an odd music venue. The stage faces the bar with a thin row of seats, and there is seating to the sides either toward the door or back by the kitchen on the main floor and along a balcony upstairs. Sound carries best to the balcony, and there are a few great seats overlooking the stage. There is no drink minimum in the balcony; worst area to waitress. I do bring Rochelle on a date to hear Tracy Nelson. I can't relax fully there because I am not important enough to get drinks gratis. I do hear the bands do their sound checks in the late afternoon. I love the informal live sounds. After 5 p.m., I sit at the bar. If Alfred is there, I drink. The guitar pickers tune up, and the singers run back and forth to the telephones.

Thomas has a girlfriend on the wait staff. She is the top waitress and gets the best tables. She also coordinates the Monday tryout nights using the stage name Lulu Birmingham. Lulu, Christian, and Thomas are tight. Alfred mutters about this "dangerous" triangle, gives me a knowing eye. As the days are heating into summer, we see less and less of Thomas. On a Friday, I get to work and trot down to the basement. The office door is locked, which means nothing. I knock. Laden with heavy Shakespearean fervor, Thomas exclaims, "Hold off, Bob!" Feeling every bit a walk-off actor, I go back to the bar. Alfred is delightedly dancing around behind the bar. I repeat Thomas's strange roar. Alfred's eyes glow with anticipation. Something is about to happen. Suddenly Thomas charges by the bar and through the revolving door. Spit back onto Fifth Avenue, he storms by the bay windows. I never see him again.

I take a long weekend and do not come back until Wednesday. The great purge is already accomplished. It turns out Thomas has been embezzling the operation and in fact is not even an owner. He juggles other investors to cover his unfunded share.

Thomas and his friends Lulu and Christian are out. Shortly before this climatic third act upheaval, a new cook is hired. Ross Wisdom actually comes from Austin. Ross is suddenly the head cook. New waitresses are brought on and the club continues normally except for in the office. The old accountant colluded with Thomas so a new accountant is hired. All the books have to be reconstructed back to the beginning. McGivney is around all the time. Thomas comes in one night and tries to strangle Tony, but Mort pulls him off. The club secures a police order to keep him away. The Lone Star is forced to cut back to save its ass. The restaurant no longer opens for lunch. The afternoons are dead, and I am taken off meaningless duties. Now my work actually relates to the health of the business. It makes sense that I was hired as a bookkeeper without a decimal point of knowledge on the subject.

I am asked to come in on a full-time basis. Rochelle and I have just moved into a larger and more expensive apartment. The increase in hours will help this transition over the summer months. I arrive each morning at 9 a.m.: open up the doors, take in the mail, check the answering machine, start my new clerical chores. Tony comes in a few hours later. The job sparks my creativity. I get up at seven each morning to write poetry. This is my form of scamming the system on work. By the time I am out my own door, I have done my day's real work. I walk west on 11th street to the windy corner at Second Avenue. There is St. Mark's Church; I walk brushing its iron wrought fence with my hand. Here is Gene, the sextant, taking garbage to the street. Wave. At Third Avenue and 12th Street, I check out which ladies of the night are still working the before-work johns. West of Fourth Avenue, the neighborhood changes to fancy, except for Broadway. She holds her own, not fancy, not dingy, just busy. The Strand bookstore is dragging its old wooden book tables out onto the sidewalk.

University Place quietly assaults the senses with small French restaurants and tasty charcuteries. Fifth Avenue looms ahead like marble statues. I feel a worldly pride knowing I have the keys in my pocket to open up a Fifth Avenue storefront. The broad avenue's sun drenches beautiful men and women going to work; I am lifted out any leftover doldrums from the day before. The Lone Star shines like a silver dollar on the corner. I peer into the darkened recesses of the bar and see a tiny amber light illuminate the cash register and dirty tablecloths. I can smell the stale odor of beer before I slip the key in the door and open it. Entering, I can tell how well the club did the night before by the extent of the disarray. I start up the bar coffeemaker and take a cup, after adding a dollop of fine Irish whiskey, to sit at the bar and sort mail. I enjoy the afternoon much less. Mort is here. The phones ring. Heated club issues build up under the afternoon sun. At five o'clock I sign out as the Lone Star opens for happy hour. I pause at the bar for a gin and tonic to transport me home.

The ambience of a nightclub is rush and last-minute frenzy. Each day surpasses the last with new hassles: missing deliveries, insistent creditors, breaking machines, fuming musicians, empty larders. I don't mind being sent out to purchase a new microphone or deliver a rent check as late as humanly possible. Often I am handed the telephone and told to stall a guy who is demanding payment: "You see, the accountants handle all that now." They take my name and when the check does not arrive, they call back asking for me. I change my tack, and become indignant (blame the boss) that the payment is not paid. "I will personally look into this and get back to you, ASAP." I do go to bat for creditors, and I juggle the payments as long as I need to. At first, lying on the telephone is odious to me, but I find it gets easier as I get lots of opportunities at the club.

More changes are brewing. Alfred is being groomed to be a new manager. The new accountant comes in. He is a child-like man named Beanblatt. He's arrogant and demanding, he imposes a new ultra-complicated accounting system. Tony breaks out in a rash as he spends hours every day on the forms. Beanblatt spends long hours in the office. He treats me with open contempt. He tells me to bring him a hamburger, which I do. He yells, "Hey, how about a napkin, fella!" I know how to work with Mort's chaotic record keeping. He writes on tiny scraps of paper that get lost in piles on his desk. I know Mort's habits and can retrieve his scraps as well as locate important corporate documents. Beanblatt discovers that Mort is useless to him; he softens his contempt for me to a milder disdain. Everybody hates Beanblatt and his arcane accounting procedures. So much money has been stolen and so much information has been covered up that we all have to endure his absolute dictatorship.

Ross Wisdom is a pretty good cook, although not the fastest; his food strongly resembles restaurant food. I am chatting with Ross in the kitchen; we discuss the high cost of the Fifth Avenue operation. I lump together all the expenses, such as rent, payroll, utilities, payoffs to inspectors, advertising, insurance, etc., and call it overhead. Ross looks up from fifty pounds of raw cow that he is pounding into burgers and says, "That is not overhead." He explains that that overhead is the constant expense that it not affected by being open for business or not. The rent is overhead, but not the payroll. Ross tells me he has a degree in accounting. I am dumbfounded, "We should change places! They need you in the office." "No way! I like it up here and I want to cook."

I like to go out the revolving door onto Fifth Avenue and look downtown; see cars driving through heat waves around the arch in Washington Square. Uptown I see the purpling haze of exhaust fumes filling Midtown. Standing on the border of east and west, which is soft loam between skyscrapers uptown and downtown bedrock, I look straight up into the clear sky. Everything I see is overhead.

McGivney is going nuts; oppressed with cost cutting, he likes to fire people. If a waitress is a little bit surly to him, she is out the next day. He is in every respect the opposite of Mort; he is a perfectionist, which is a terrible trait to have in the nightclub business. It is Mort who embodies the Lone Star body and soul, from his ash-stained dirty denim vest to his false Texan garrulousness. He expertly plays people off one another and remains a slob. He sleeps on the stage several days running and starts to smell. People turn their heads away when he speaks to them. In the morning, after I awaken him from his cuddly sleep wrapped around a drum set, he alternately tells me his woes and then jokes as he coffees up. He tells me of his pain:

THE PAIN getting the club going.

THE PAIN the investors give him when they have to reinvest.

THE PAIN McGivney gives him every day.

THE PAIN he sells them on Thomas; now they don't trust him.

THE PAIN the club suffered a five-month financial setback.

THE PAIN Tony isn't any good; the waitresses are all *schleps*.

THE PAIN the bartender isn't fast enough.

THE PAIN   the cook isn't fat enough.

THE PAIN Mort covers his face and mutters.

Surprisingly at this point, Mort's bookings are getting better. I feel secure with him now. He is in the liquor storeroom (which houses the telephone junction box) with a musician; they are smoking a joint. Telephone repairmen arrive and I send them in. Mort comes out steaming mad, but he can't do anything to me. I overhear someone mention Mort's toupee. I am stunned that I have not noticed it before. Now it is the only thing I see on Mort's bald head. He finds his way into my poetry:

> if he picks it up
>> he puts it down
>>>>> somewhere else
> if he has an elbow to place
>> it's in my face
> if his breath is blue eggs
>> he directly speaks
>> he calls me usurper
> he thinks I throw his scraps out
> he teaches me to sell a menu
>> from the top down
> he is growing pale
>>>> coming down
> with a cold
> under his toupee
> his burger needs flipping
> to me it's Bobby
> to others it's
> tell whatshisface

I am told that photographers from Purple magazine are coming today. "These will be nudies." Mort says. The male model arrives first, then the make-up people, the set designer, and the lighting and camera people. Lastly arrive the female models. The windows are covered with tablecloths, and the set is lit.

The male model is an old-time bartender, and the females are cowgirls at the bar. Beanblatt throws me out of the office, so I migrate to a table on the balcony with my papers. The women at the bar have an argument and throw their drinks on each other. The bartender is just watching with lascivious delight. After a few rolls of film, the women are wrestling naked, and the purple segments are about to begin. The porters stop mopping; Mort puts down the receiver; the dishwashing machine finishes its cycle; I put down my garbanzo bean salad; Beanblatt comes up from below. The ladies eat out each other's toes, tits, and pussies. Then it is over; the women retire to the dressing room to find their clothes. The Lone Star tingles with an excited male voyeuristic air that dissipates when the women return to the bar for a real drink in their own attire. Beanblatt is transported; he floats through the door. The next day, he is still beaming as he declares that he will not charge for the day before! "Boy, that brunette was nice!"

Alfred is working hard to become a perfect manager. He creates a source book and fills it with all the information needed to run the bar. He is chastened as soon he starts the job; it means harder work, longer hours, less pay. Alfred realizes that any improvement he could possibly make would be undone by Mort. After managing The Biggest Honky-tonk North of Abilene for one week, Alfred quits to avoid a full nervous breakdown. By summer's end, Tony is looking haggard. He bears the weight for the club not turning a profit even with better bookings and larger audience. Suddenly, a death in Tony's family means he is gone for two weeks. I am managing: ordering food, making up the cash register bank for the night, taking in bank deposits, doing inventory, overseeing work schedules, handling squabbles. During this hard week I tell Mort that I can't do it without more money. I am promised to be taught the full accountant program and that I will get a raise. "Just hold on, Bobby," Mort pleadingly lies. "Soon we will be able to do right by everyone; just wait a few more weeks."

I learn a lot this week and almost feel like a boss. McGivney is in the office; hysterical about the size of the payroll, he puts his evil eye on me and tells me to fire two of the waitress this morning. "Or else," he adds. He leaves the office. Some part of me realizes that this has gone too far. Some part of me also wants to experience firing somebody. But without any thinking further about why I am so ready to do another person's dirty work, I call the first waitress and tell her how it is. I am calling to fire her. Management is fucked up. Turns out she didn't like the job and isn't sore about it. The second waitress I call does care and is outraged. Playing the part of a total worm, I agree and advise her not to settle for it. She does fight for her job and gets to keep it. I learn that when I fire people who make more money than I do, I am morally done for. I feel sick in my gut as if I informed on my parents.

When they need to fire one cook, Eddie he tells me, "They always fire the cook with a beard." Bearded Eddie is right. Then they fire Ross. He is speechlessly hurt. Service is king. The best waitresses are too important to a nightclub to fire. Because of these non-service firings, I get the strong feeling that I am next. After one gives too much; he is of no further use. I need a vacation.

In September, Fifth Avenue changes her dress from summer running outfits to classy autumn evening dresses. The Lone Star finally settles on someone to take Thomas's place. If he is honest, there will be no room for me. McGivney brings his wife in to learn my chores. She is volunteering her time. Tony had told me he would warn me about changes in my job status, tells me my job is in danger. Mort is nowhere to be seen. I keep thinking about all of his promises to keep me working above my grade. He avoids me all week. On Friday, the new boss takes me down to the office, and says he has wants to lay me off. The Lone Star will not contest my getting unemployment compensation. As much as I am not surprised, I do go into shock. I list my strong points and what I feel I achieved at the Lone Star. "I formed a working relationship with Mort." He concedes that is something and asks me for my keys.

I am sitting at the Lone Star bar having a triple strength gin and tonic. I have an appropriated bottle of Tanqueray gin to see me through the night. The new boss comes up to shake my hand in apology one more time. He notices the bottle at my feet and chooses not to say anything. I tell Nancy that I am fired. She is outraged and rails against the management. But how can I kick? I am or was a part of that management. I do feel dirty from the shame of being so thoroughly used. The alcohol is taking over. Alfred is gone, Christian is gone, Ross is gone, Thomas is gone, Lulu is not here. Tony is going fast. The funny thing is that after that terrible summer, the Lone Star does finally take off.

IV

A few weeks before I get laid off at the Lone Star, Rochelle starts to hint that she might be pregnant. Even the mere possibility of pregnancy makes me see children everywhere. I notice babies in the bank, children bawling in the supermarket, grade-schoolers racing circles around me. Everywhere kids, kids, kids. I come home and find Rochelle sitting at her desk in the sun-drenched studio. I stand in her doorway and she turns to me with an ultra-quizzical expression, "Guess what, Bob!" I look at her now with new regard. "I am glad," I stammer. [I was taught to read using a whole word method that employs a method of word associations rather than phonetic sounding out. My mother tells me that when I saw the word *glad* I read it as *happy*.] I mean to tell Rochelle that I am happy. This change in the offing inures me to the discomfort to being let go at the club. The larger labors ahead make unemployment income look like a good idea. As I wait for the checks to start, Rochelle and I walk over to Ben's Baby Furniture on Avenue A to ogle cribs in a state of bewilderment. During this second honeymoon, I receive a notice to appear for jury duty.

The timing seems perfect. Here are two weeks of work that hold the distinct glamour of distributing justice. I also see it as an opportunity to do some reading and get paid $13 a day. Jury duty is a service, and I believe that I want to be on a jury because I would want me on the jury if I were the defendant. I don't see it as work; I should know better. It costs money to work: commuting, lunching, buying clothes, fueling on alcohol and coffee. Working bears its own cost. I am an idiot to assume that jury duty wouldn't also demand a penance be paid.

Early on a Monday morning I report to the New York State Supreme Court Building at 60 Centre Street for jury duty. There are many women and retired men assembling. We are ushered into the great rotunda and told that we were all headed up to the Criminal Courts at 100 Centre no choice. The Criminal Courts are housed in a monolithic gray building that sits on and squashes the old cesspool of the Five Points, twenty stories tall and two blocks long. The central jury room is on the fifteenth floor. The drab hall has many rows of hard benches that are already littered with despondent Gothamites. An officer sits at a big high desk speaking to people without looking down on them. The benches are decidedly uncomfortable enough to make one want to get on a jury rather than spend two weeks in here. They have the first jury call; the names of fifty prospective jurors are pulled out of a drum to go down the hall to Part 46 and sit on the visitor benches. I am among them. The court has a high ceiling and windows near the top that let in some natural light. The walls are wood paneled and darkly stained with justice. The judge's imposing bench fills the front of the court with the weight of the state.

The bailiff, the defendants with their lawyers, and the prosecutor enter stage right. Everyone sitting stands up as the judge ascends her perch. She has short hair and a lively smile; leans over her desk to explain jury selection to the prospective jurors. Twelve people are selected to fill the jury box, then the lawyers and the judge question them. After this first dozen is processed there are only two filled-juror chairs. This is obviously a lengthy process; we are supposed to remain alert and attentive to the proceedings. Just before lunch, my name is pulled out of the drum; I get to sit in the jury box with its cushioned seats.

George Schneeman tells me he recently had jury duty after decades of avoidance. He ducks getting on any jury by refusing to agree to follow all the judge's instructions. I am beginning to like the courtroom and the judge. I feel comfortable. I am guilty of something. What if I end up at the defendant's table? Yes, I want to be judged by poets, and further assume that occupation poet is a sure dismissal from any jury. Judge Gable asks each of us if we are married and what magazines we read. She smiles and is very pleasant, much like a politician among voters, which is what she is. Mister Public Attorney is verbose and distracted. The judge has to stop him from going on and on. Mister Anisi, the New York State attorney is a young doll in a trim suit and bright oxblood red shoes. He is soft-spoken, a bit hesitant, and likeable. I realize that this is his first case. The judge questions me a little bit about being a poet. "That must be interesting." She doesn't ask if I am married. Mister Public Attorney asks if I have ever been the victim of a crime. I tell about the time I was mugged at knifepoint in a Midtown elevator. He asks if I think I have become prejudiced by the experience. "Just toward elevators." Mr. Anisi asks what the subject matter of my poetry is. I am stunned.

The insanity of the entire situation dawns on me, "At this moment I am more concerned with forms of poetry rather than subject." Anisi clarifies, "Like sonnet form, like free verse. . ." "Yes, something like that." He asks me if I am published. "Sure. My wife and I publish small-press poetry books." Mr. Public Attorney perks up, "A wife. I don't think this has been mentioned before." He shoots a little victory glance at the Judge. Anisi asks me what my wife does? "She is a filmmaker, graphic artist, writer, part-time secretary." I want to bring Rochelle into the jury box with me. The lawyers confer; to my utter dismay, I am not asked to leave the box. Two other jurors and I are escorted out the side door that leads to the jury deliberation room.

The jury room opens; several previously chosen jurors snap their attention to us. We join them at the large wooden table surrounded by clunky mismatched wooden chairs. We share what we know about the trial procedures and avoid discussing the case. I am in the second group; there are still the majority and alternates to choose. This will take days. The walls are plain green and unadorned by pictures. I imagine portraits of former judges to make one remember to follow the instructions. There are two bathrooms. The jury room faces northeast. The Manhattan Bridge looms large, with the upper reaches of the Williamsburg Bridge close by. I can see the Con Edison plant on 14th Street at the river, the telephone building at 13th Street and Second Avenue. I start to read; whenever the court adjourns, we are allowed to leave for a set amount of time. Sometimes I go down to the lobby to watch the eclectic groups of the accused and lawyers mixing together. Other times, I slip out the back door of 100 Centre, which opens to Columbus Park and Chinatown. One block away a cart of live fish is being bustled along the sidewalk; junkies are scoring in the park; kids are playing stickball in front of their school. I walk back to my fifteenth floor confinement past bright palettes of oranges and leafy greens. At the end of the third day the judge pops into the jury room, announces, "Mr. Rosenthal, you will be interested to know that also on this jury is the director of the American Academy of Poets." She quickly leaves; the jurors turn to me, demanding to know what the judge just said. I hardly know.

The jury is getting interesting. There is: June, an editor for a medical journal; Ollie, an efficiency expert and the only African American on the panel; Joyce, an x-ray technician; Shirley, a housewife; Tom, upstate tree farmer; Dick, a waiter / scriptwriter; Paula, the forelady and career businesswoman; Betty Kray, the director of the American Academy of Poets; Sandy, stay-at-home mom; Donna, a grade school teacher. And there is me and one other who is evaporated from memory. Betty Kray is real fun. She brings in literary maps of Lower Manhattan that show the city as it was for Walt Whitman or Edgar Allan Poe. We walk these streets with her in the lead during breaks. Soon the entire jury likes one another. Everyone is intellectual and friendly. Long stories are bandied about, mutual acquaintances are found, sexual preferences are hinted at. I get the impression that the other two men are gay. I read with both ears open.

On the first day of the second week of jury service, the entire jury is seated in the courtroom, and sworn in; the trial begins. The charge is attempted robbery. The defendants are Calvin King and Vincent Lisbon. They are accused of attempting to rob another young man, Lee Jones (they are classmates), on the eighteenth floor of the Polo Grounds housing project. It is Jones who originally presses charges. It only takes two days; one of the days is taken up with challenges. I begin to dislike the public defender, Mr. Bogus, more and more. He makes redundant speeches with a preposterous pompousness. Judge Gable has to stop him in rude terms to get him to shut up. He comically flops back into his chair. The only evidence in the case is the first-hand testimony of Jones. He proves to be a terrible witness. He is hard to hear; he is so hesitant that his story seems vague and, worse, improbable. We understand that these boys with a gun threaten him for fifteen minutes. Lee seems believable, but it remains impossible to construct his story. Unfortunately, Mr. Anisi is not able to pinpoint the story either. Before being sent into deliberation, the judge charges the jury. She reminds us that intent can be proved two ways; through conscious planning (hard to prove in court) or through inference from concrete (proved) actions.

Intent does prove to be the hang-up for most of the jurors. Although we feel the defendants are guilty of something, the problem is that it is hard to find a concrete action that proves intent to steal. Originally, the charges had been assault, but those are dropped. Everyone feels that assault seems the better charge, but we don't understand yet that assault can only be proved with medical evidence. There are two charges to rule on: attempted armed robbery and attempted robbery. I question myself closely and realize that the only vote I can make is not guilty beyond a reasonable doubt. On the first ballot we are split eight not guilty and four guilty. It is early afternoon; we start to make our arguments. I know that deliberation would start that Thursday. I assume that we would be done by the end of day; I don't tell Rochelle that there is a possibility of being sequestered, because I don't believe it can happen in this case. As soon as we start to debate, the bailiff comes in for our lunch orders. It takes fifteen minutes for the pad to go around the table. The state pays for the lunch, but we each have to put in a quarter tip for the delivery person. The afternoon gets old; the food comes. We eat and discuss the case. We vote again and this time it is ten not guilty. The lateness of the day might bring the holdouts around. At about 6:30 the bailiff tells us that the state is taking us out to dinner. We are walked over to an Irish Pub; we can order a nice dinner the state buys and one alcoholic drink that we pay for ourselves. I have grilled red snapper, minestrone, salad, cheesecake and one Old Grand-Dad on the rocks. We are told to leave a dollar tip each. I want to call Rochelle but we are not allowed any phone calls. The bailiff tells me that he will call my wife, but he won't say when. He doesn't call until 11pm. I am worried about and protective of Rochelle; feeling pangs of expectant fatherhood, yet here I am eating a swell supper. I sit across from Joyce, one of the holdouts. I tell her that I support not guilty from the deepest part of my heart and not because I am following someone else's argument. On the way out, I cop a dinner roll and stuff it in my pocket. When we get back to the jury room, we vote again. Joyce has changed her vote leaving only one holdout left. Judge Gable comes into our room and says that she and the lawyers want to go home; the jury is to be bound over to the Ramada Inn for the night. Everyone feels like shit.

A very ordinary MTA bus is waiting for us in front of 100 Centre. The twelve jurors and three bailiffs climb aboard barely filling the large bus. I sit next to Ollie and we whisper about who we think the holdout is. We are both sure it is Donna. Our first stop is Whalen's Drugstore at the corner Sixth Avenue and West 8th Street. We buy toothpaste, razors, candy, and I buy shoelaces and cheap cigars. I am plotting about the room assignments. I know there will be two to a room, except for the odd person in each gender. The two other guys seem interested in each other; Tom asks me how I feel about the rooms. I say I want the single room. Ollie, being the single African American woman, also volunteers for the single room. The bus drives uptown through the Eighth Avenue pornography district and stops at the Ramada Inn. A few flights up, I am let into my own orange room with orange curtains and green bloated lamps. The windows look onto an empty warehouse and will not open. The cable TV advertises movies to watch for a fee, but we are not allowed to do this. Broadcast TV offers only episodes of *The Honeymooners*. While I munch on my purloined roll, put on my new shoelaces, smoke a cigar, I watch the episode where Alice gets a little puppy and Ralph will not let her keep it. She hides the dog and keeps it a secret. Ralph brings Norton home and brags about Alice's delicious dip. Ralph pulls what he thinks is Alice's dip from the fridge. We in TV land know it is really dog food. The boys eat a lot of dip, Ralph says that the dip is so good that he can market it and make a million dollars. Soon Norton spies an empty dog food can, and Ralph flips out. He finds the dog and threatens to take it to the pound. Norton says, "You've lost your membership in the human race!" This is exactly how I feel being cut off from my family. I peek into the hall to see if there is really a guard posted in the hall, and there is. I smoke another cigar in the bathtub. I read *Brilliant Corners* magazine with an interview with Paul Carroll, who talks about slapping Allen Ginsberg. I read poems by Anselm Hollo, and I read the chapter on eternity in *Allen Verbatim*. I slumber off hugging a pillow next to me.

The bailiffs awaken us at seven in the morning. The jurors assemble and go down together to breakfast at the motel's cafe. I sit with Betty, Tom, and June. The eggs are processed but the potatoes are real. Betty talks about her father shooting pheasant from their living room window in West Texas. I talk about a film I have seen that shows a scrambled egg factory, endless eggs being dropped down a tube. June asks me to stop. Tom and I discuss solar and wind energy possibilities. We board our MTA bus and head back downtown; as we ride down Fifth Avenue, people try hard to hail us by stepping out into the streets and shake their fists at us when we don't stop. This day is a strong déjà vu because we are all dressed exactly as we are the day before. Friday morning is gloomy. Nobody wants to go back to the Ramada Inn for the weekend.

As soon as we are back in our seats, we have to order lunch and leave a tip. Fifteen minutes later, we start to make our statements again and take a vote; there is still one guilty. Each time it is my turn to speak, I essentially give the same speech but use more abstract metaphors to illustrate my philosophy. I invoke the geometry of the reasoning we were asked to do. We are charged by the law to approach the case from a certain angle, and if we have any doubts, we are not obliged to go further looking for guilt not included in the charge against the defendants. I think of guilt and innocence as a continuum rather than moral absolutes. Betty likes my talks. Other jurors discuss race, "Boys will be boys," scientifically, hypothetically "it could have happened this way." Tom demonstrates a hammerlock on me in which it only appears as if he is going through my pockets. Donna admits that she is the holdout and says, " I just believe these boys are guilty." We have to restrain ourselves from jumping on her to question her belief. Donna enjoys the attention; some jurors psychoanalyze her for free.

By lunch, I am feeling trapped and a little insane. I start to jog around the table; Betty joins me. We jog a long time; breathing deeply and throwing our arms about. We are channeling our Victorian concept of being healthy. By midafternoon, with everyone exhausted, we head back into the courtroom to hear Judge Gable explain again how intent is established in law. We also have Lee Jones's testimony read by the court reporter. We've already decided what we needed to hear in it to convict. We can actually hear the testimony better now; we do not hear the necessary language. We get back to the jury room and Donna switches her vote to not guilty. The sign of relief from all is dashed when we vote on the lesser charge. Still one guilty! Everyone looks at Donna, but it is Shirley who sputters, "Well, they're guilty of something!" Everyone roars at once. Forelady Paula, a champion of Aesthetic Realism, reestablishes order, and we try to reason with Shirley by explaining that if intent is not proven on one charge, it cannot be proved in the lesser charge. Shirley just shrugs her shoulders and repeats, "I just feel that they should be guilty of something!" Soon the afternoon sky starts to darken; Shirley understands she cannot hold out longer; changes her vote.

Paula hands the verdict to the judge, who glances at it and scowls as she reads it out loud. The defendants' friends cheer and are gaveled silent. The jury is dismissed. As we head back to the jury room for our coats, we talk to the judge and the lawyers. Judge Gable tells us everything that we were not allowed to be told before deciding. "These are the worst kind of kids!" We find out that each young man has previous convictions for robbery, and one has an open case in the Bronx on the same charge. Mr. Anisi tells us that Lee Jones was reluctant to testify because his family was being threatened in the Polo Grounds. The day of delay was because police had to be sent to escort him and force him to testify. Mr. Anisi did say this was his first trial and that it had only been given to him the day before it opened. He admits that it was a weak case and should not have been brought to trial. Someone asks about the jury selection; he says he wanted a smart jury. "Oh, no you don't!" Shirley says. ""I don't?" "Aw naw, they intellectualize too much." Shirley is surely right.

I decline to go for a drink with the other jurors; I try to leave as quickly as possible. Mr. Bogus wants my thoughts on the case; I yell something about going home at him. He says, "Aw OK, forget about it." I feel terrible. Those kids seem guilty; even though I know that, I let them off. Even if justice is blind, it is not always correct. I go home and lie down in bed as the sun sets in the back windows. Rochelle comes home but doesn't see me in the dark; I call out to her. She is as startled as if I have just returned from war. She runs over and jumps on me sobbing. I feel like I have committed a crime. I must be guilty of something. Rochelle feels just a little heavier. I vow I will rip up the next jury summons I get; that's only a misdemeanor.

V

The nature of cycles is that they complete themselves. I quit cleaning houses where dishonesty is justified. Look for work where effort is defeating. Land a bookkeeping job where the boss is dishonest. I am used up and squeezed out. I am called upon to do a civic duty to discover that my honesty is misbegotten. It is better to self and body to stay clear of the commerce in the world. Like Thoreau, just plant one's own row of beans. He lifts his head every time he hears the train to Boston chug by Walden Pond taking people to look for work. It is the writer in him that creates the austerity of his wisdom. It is that other person in me who at all times knows what his work is. How untrammeled it is. How agreeable it is to do, no matter the difficulty. More and more people realize that they are living in the world. Yet they work in a multitude of ways to forget it. I walk up Fifth Avenue and see the success and pollution of society, as it is one and the same. Look overhead, see a purpling sky. I know I can't take it with me; it takes me with it. It is my work that remains.

Something all people build for themselves.

A Place and a Time

"... a place and a time in
which, rich or poor, you were
stuck together in the misery
(and the freedom) of the
place, where not even money
could insulate you."

– Edmund White

Take a Walk on the Wild Side

1972, I am driving Ted Berrigan to a poetry reading in Detroit. Anne and Ken
Mikolowski are the sponsors. On the way to Detroit we stop in Ann Arbor to see
Donald Hall. Donald and Ted visit; Ted goes to the bathroom. After we climb back into
my red VW Squareback, Ted pulls out his find: Valium! He gives me my first one ever as
we merge onto the interstate toward the Motor City.

The day is fading when we pull into the Detroit ghetto. Ted has no idea where the
Mikolowskis live. He tells me to pull over and wait in the car; he steps out into the
brightly lit street. Ted disappears into a liquor store that is a Plexiglas box. I wait at
the wheel. The blue Valium is washing over me in deep sapphire tones of night. The
FM rock radio puts on a song I hear for the first time. Lou Reed sings "Take a Walk
on the Wild Side." The world is surreal: the glass broken in the street, the lithium
vapor streetlights reflecting off the pavement, a neon-sign flashing LIQUOR. Danger
surrounds me. Lou's calm voice and his backup choir buoy me with its insistence that
the wild side is where comfort is. Before Ted pulls the car door open, my life is forever
changed.

Want to Read?

I already know Bob Holman from Chicago. Now he is in New York City, living with
Patricia Kirby on the Upper West Side. He and I go to St. Mark's Church to attend a
Monday night reading. The Wednesday readings are the premier readings. The Monday
series tilts toward performance. Bob and I meet Ed Freidman, who is scheduling and
running the series. We tell Ed that we are writing a play and would like to perform
it. Ed, without missing a beat, offers us a date for the next month. The genius of Ed's

programing is that the Monday readings have spontaneous energy that allows poets to experiment and go overboard.

The first Monday of every month is an open reading. By 8 p.m. forty poets have signed up to read, the night of three-minute readings starts. The audience is made up of the other readers. It is a tough group that appreciates both the good writing and the bad. But, one has to be totally good or pretty bad. This is a chance to take out a new poem and give it voice. Hear the poem bounce off the Parish Hall walls. The reception is unimportant. In a very real way, the open reading is more nerve-wracking than a full reading. It is a great way to practice channeling nervous energy into a clear voice that can carry the room. It is at an open reading that I hear a young poet, my age, read a poem with a vigorous cadence and a highly developed image bank. I get excited and run up to him to tell him how much I enjoy his stuff. He tells me that he likes my poem too. Smiling with a shy hesitant grin, I meet a new poet friend, Michael Scholnick.

Many types of writers flock to read at these unscripted events: Schoolteachers from New Jersey flaunt a sexual power they can't express at the day job; frustrated old poets read despite their feelings of bitterness; eccentric poets become legion. Billy Wertzel writes and reads only rhyming doggerel. A. A. Pritchard, the author of a collection of poems called *Death's Teat*, clutches the wooden podium and pulls it apart in his zeal, Michael Dissent, whose book is *Stomping the Goyem*, rails against anyone who dares to obstruct him on the sidewalks. Bernard Whitelaw Alphabet and Olson McIntyre orate to the heavens over Second Avenue.

I join a generation of poets by attending the readings at the Poetry Project. We sit together on the table under the della Robbia at the rear of the Parish Hall. We laugh a lot and make our friends feel like great poets. The New York City audience snickers with gusto but also listens with a scary intensity that can unnerve a visiting poet used to audience inattention. Jim Brodey, Michael Scholnick, Gary Lenhart, Steve Levine, Simon Schuchat, Susan Cataldo, Susie Timmons, Eileen Myles, Lenny Goldstein, Michael Sappol, Steve Hamilton, Ed Friedman, Tom Savage, Bob Holman, David Herz, Rochelle Kraut, Susan Dubelyew, Jeff Wright, Charlotte Carter, Greg Masters, Tom Wiegel, George-Thérèse Dickenson, Tom Carey, Simon Pettet, John Godfrey, Yuki Hartman, form a phalanx of serious poet friends who share their reading of poetry, their performances, their publications, their parties, and the drama of their love affairs.

After the reading, go to The Orchidia at Ninth Street for beer and pizza. The poet who just read and has a paycheck buys the pizza with everything, except if Jim Brodey is the reader; he checks out of the bar before the bill comes.

I am regularly going to the Wednesday reading series at the Poetry Project. The nave of the church has drab old pews with high backs. One can lie down and disappear or read the Bible without being conspicuous. In 1975, I start to take impressionistic notes during the readings. The deep dark pews easily hide many things. I hide a notebook there and madly scribble notes throughout the readings. I note down lines I like and describe the way each poet reads their works. I pay close attention to how the poets tell the audience that they are about to read their concluding poem. My favorite is Ed Marshall: "I will break on this one." When I hear Michael McClure, his reading style distracts me. I am a new poet on the scene and do not consider my opinion carefully. My New York School cool hears vanity. I describe his poetry as "a waterfall on foam rubber." I love this snarky metaphor and don't give it any more thought. I am usually more concerned with the atmosphere at the reading rather than just the poetry. My notes were published in the World Magazine #30. Some examples:

Nov. 5, 1975 MICHAEL RUMAKER & ED MARSHALL

Mike Rumaker, What people think I could become if they can only see me where I am. Not truly. Either I am paranoid no I am not. Well I know I am not looking at life from the point of view of a comb. The easy unbreakable drawl. More example of Going to Church St. Mark's Church Readings. Anne Waldman looking back to the door. Larry Fagin is here showing how it is done: sit with forehead resting on fist-devote! Mike gives away his best lines by making mistakes. "one good short poem, four good lines" Rochelle Kraut SONG FOR WHALES after he "wets his whistle" Mmm Mmm Mm M Mm. Reading Hoppers wear sweaters & slacks. Larry tells Mike "You were terrific! Terrific!" Ed Marshall precise hairline. "To Emerson" his first words. Larry is unseen. Yuki Hartman is writing his poems: Yuki's poems are so long that he must write them all the time, that way they are long as Yuki is. Young man leaves and rattles doors. Larry walks down the aisle, "He's great!" Rochelle turns to me and says, "He is great!" "Did you hear of Olson? There is an L in his name too." You really can't read the Prayer Book. Rochelle laughs at "Styles From Yale" Styles is O.W. Holmes' father-in-law. Ed uses all-purpose line while searching for place, "Fee Fi Fo Fum I smell the blood of an Englishman!" "Yes, say it in your nose, Olson." "Allen Ginsberg knew I had more up there than I put down on paper." "Metropolitan Victrolas" Young man comes back as old fat man. "I will break on this one."

Dec. 3, 1975 MICHAEL McCLURE

Tonight Show patter, plugs books thinks advertising "My friend, Gary Synder." Steve Malmude walks out. Poems sound like a waterfall on foam rubber. Video machine is on meaning here Anne Waldman Michael Brownstein "crickets' eyes between the verses of song" I was covering a Bob Dylan? Concert? "They moved tons of equipment." "All conceptions of boundaries are lies." I would say lines. "This poem was written at the highest train pass in the world." "This poem was written about an experience in Peru. First line is from Lenin." "Shanty restaurant in Bogatá." Each poem is a description of feelings with ideas about words. Break Anti-chamber. Neil Hackman says, "I used to write like that." Neil loves it. Charles Bernstein wonders (sometimes) where they find the people who read here.

A decade later, I am sitting at Allen's desk on East 12th street. Allen brings up Michael McClure. Allen introduces me to Michael and goes into the kitchen. Michael comes up to me and exclaims, "You wrote that review in the World!" I instantly know what he is referring to. I sit sheepishly as he steps up behind me and puts both arms around me. His hands hold a volume of his poems in front of me. I am trapped. Michael starts to read his poems. His finger points to each word as he magnificently intones them. He reads several poems and I know he is about to read the entire volume. I blurt out, "Michael, you are a really great poet!" We are both laughing as he releases me.

I make sure to see Taylor Mead in Michael's marvelous play *Spider Rabbit*. I listen to Michael's growling on old recordings and find a place in my head for his call.

Decades later, around 2010, Allen is gone. Michael and his wife Amy stay in what we still call Edith's room when visiting New York City. I finish the first draft of *Straight Around Allen* and leave it for Michael to peruse. The next day, Michael is horrified, shocked at the very first paragraph. He tells me I put a hex on my own work!

My initial paragraph is very poetic. I reference W.B. Yeats' *A Vision*. But it ends like this, "Allen Ginsberg with his prodigious intelligence and vast memory of verses seems to need a deliberate fellow to follow him like the man in a circus sweeping up behind the elephant. Am I born to be that fellow?"

Michael assures me that this fecal metaphor is horrible. I try to assure him that I mean to show ironic humility. But McClure won't hear it, he only sees my vanity!

I rework this image; it takes weeks of thinking. I move the revised paragraph a little deeper into the book, "In W.B. Yeats' *A Vision*, I am a phase four of the moon. In Yeats' schema for the fourth phase, the beginnings of ambition are present but not their attainment. I am primary in focus not secondary. I seem to have a kind of wisdom that is practical not abstract, as Yeats says, 'a wisdom of saws and proverbs.' Allen Ginsberg with his prodigious intelligence and vast memory of verses seems to need a deliberate fellow to follow him like a tiger's tail that extends and bends to create balance. I am born to be that fellow."

I work on the book for nine more years. It finally comes out in 2019. I include Michael in my acknowledgements and send him a copy. Weeks later, Michael mails me a note, which is now framed over my desk. Michael is in front of me all the time.

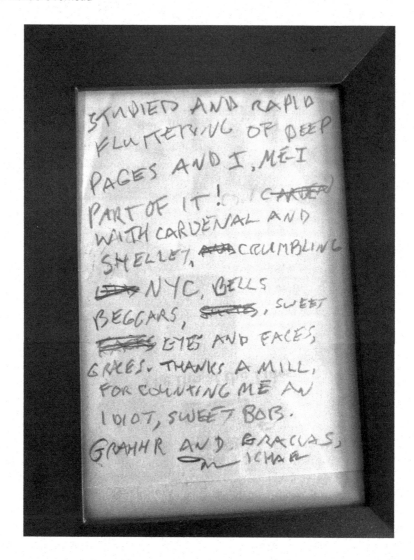

Mar, 31, 1976 JOHN GODFREY & JIM BRODEY

 John Godfrey reads from *The Music of the Curbs*. "love poem snicker" "a slip
of the breeze two flights up." smile terse "the small of the back is so slender
and the hips blossom in handfuls" "orange ripple" "Lick for lip" a misreading.
"Moonless edges mistakenly cooked by stars" "close up with a flag waver" "shit
blast from the river echoes" Intermission, Tom Carey sings his own songs with
Neil Hackman. Simon S. asks Jim Brodey what he is going to do. Jim says,
"Ask me when you are 22," I don't think Neil knows folk music. "You always
get some lover trying to steal the show." Tom Carey "I'd have the blues too if I

wrote some of these lines." Rochelle Kraut introduces Jim Brodey. Man behind tape recorder falls off his chair. Jim reads "this is too ecumenical" Boy, this is an early work!" "A rhapsody in the pits." rubs postcard on mike for those listening to tape. "Dream of hamburger with everything; I always wanted everything." Rudy has to go. "Charles Ives comes in." "Magnified piss stains of immortal fire" reads sideways "Noh food in freezer." Noh el Coward. He makes words fall together though not all hits, it all sounds. Sitar tuning makes me feel like giving money "the man who owns all the electricity in N.Y. State lives across the lake" Ed Sanders is his father. Frank O'Hara his mother. "I will close with a couple of poems." "Four more and that will be it." "I don't show up on radar or any other day" he raises his voice from the middle of his voice "rotating on a stool."

The readings at the Poetry Project are a large living room where poets share their intelligence and their work and get to socialize. We live close by and often go to several readings a night.

Alice holds a baby, Bernadette, Rochelle, Ted in our apartment on East 11th Street. Photo, Lewis Warsh, around 1977.

The energy makes us want to create more reading series. As poets we are developing our deep listening skills. We hear poems as shapes, and the shapes, in turn, shape our poems. We learn to write fearlessly and live without regard for fame or fortune. Here is my look back at the some of the highlights of this education:

The Poetry Project: A Reckoning

New to City reading New Year's 1974 twixt Abbie Hoffman and
    Allen Ginsberg
Mimeo'ing books in office of poetry late into the night – hearing
    the organ play itself
Creating *Caveman* collaboratively composing directly to stencil
Gregory streaking at McClure reading
Performing Artaud's *Jet of Blood* and Tzara's *Gas Heart*
Collating parties for volumes of poetry and magazines in Parish Hall
Teaching Young Person's Poetry Workshop
Mopping up Patti Smith's spittle off the dais
Helping Rochelle curate a film series
Reading a set of psalms and pissing everyone off
Allen reading "Wichita Vortex Sutra" with Knitting Factory musicians
Alice's golden workshop – meeting all my friends at once
Bernadette's experimental writing workshop – discovering
    present tense
Smoking opium with Kathy Acker and floating on dais through
    New Year's reading
Larry Fagin barring the big doors against giant New Year's mob
    trying to enter (Quasimodo)
Hiding in the bathroom with Michael Scholnick to delay a Board vote
Sitting on the back table with Jim Brodey et al laughing
Reading "Our Version of Heaven" with Johnny Stanton
The big benefit canceled — holding NO READING — just fifty poets
Siamese Banana Gang demanding sign interpreters for the deaf
    (no deaf folk present)
John Wieners reading starts and finishes before 8 p.m.
Journaling all the Wednesday night readings noting Anne's noisy
    late entrances
All the Italian artists staging Da Vinci's *Last Supper*
Baby Max Corso wailing during Robert Lowell reading
    Allen orders Gregory to be a good parent and take the baby out
Cooking chili each of the last umpteen years for New Year's Day
    Benefit

Hosting Paul Auster's *Twentieth Century French Poetry* Celebration
Planting two trees in Poet's Grove and arranging new plaques
Loving John Ashbery's reading though fearing he might topple over
Rene Ricard exacting revenge through poetry
Lenny getting even with ex in film
Rochelle singing Ted's *Sonnets*
So many people come to life over Peter Stuyvesant's bones through
      poetry and prose, getting hit by cars, smoking in the yard, creating
      seemingly ephemeral books of poetry, hugging after absences,
      recovering mental health, cleaned up after addiction, returning after
      nesting, discovering new long projects, revisiting dance, and still
      here with decades of our aging, always my poetry home.

Writing Workshops

Bernadette Mayer runs an experimental writing workshop at the Poetry Project. The principal of the workshop is to create group writing in the workshop. We get a prompt and write for a short time. Then we go around the room reading what we just wrote. After everyone has read, any comments are about the new whole piece of writing that has been completed. It totally reorders my ways of thinking about writing and it blurs the writing of poetry with writing prose. I am going to graduate school at CCNY and I am writing a sizable piece about cleaning apartments for Francine du Plessix Gray in her new journalism class. I am having trouble finding a good narrative flow. I show my manuscript to Bernadette. She advises me to make it all present tense. When I do that, I am able to continue writing with great ease and finish *Cleaning Up New York* in a three-week rush. I discover that the present tense is very plastic; it can bend it to tell of the past and it leans to make a future sense. It adds immediacy to the prose, and eliminates an imposed sense of narrative control. Bernadette's husband, the poet Lewis Warsh, hears me read a piece of the book at CCNY. He offers to publish it as an Angel Hair book.

Several years after Rochelle and I move to Manhattan, Ted Berrigan and Alice Notley return to the Lower East Side. I help Alice look at a small available apartment on St. Mark's Place and approve. 1976, Alice leads a poetry-writing workshop at the Poetry Project. I attend and there meet a large group of young poets who become my friends. Whereas writing workshops in Chicago had been adversarial, Alice helps poets become colloquial and friendly. Intelligence is prized, and the poets are teaching one another by sharing as Alice smiles down on us. Not simplistic or easy, this is a high-powered poetry finishing school. The principals of the future rival poetry cliques attend Alice's workshop: the Language school and the 3rd generation New York School. How lucky I am that both Alice and Bernadette deign to kiss me; now I am a real writer.

Maybe because I am soon to become a father the Poetry Project offers me a position to lead a poetry workshop for children. The children were all preciously fun. They write great poems, and we have poetry adventures. Of course, we make an anthology of workshop poems and call it *Ain't They All Poems*. So much pleasure to speak out wrongly!

The Play's the Thing

1974: New York City has the affirming energy of a yes. People say *Yes* and an art event happens. Bob Holman and I want to write a play. We are poets and intend to create poet's theater. I have a story I spoke into a tape recorder about how gravity was created. I tell Bob the story, and Bob gets busy. He finds some windowpane acid and a giant newsprint sketchpad and a bunch of Magic Markers. We drop the acid at my St. Mark's Place studio apartment. As the acid is starting to arrive, we walk to Tompkins Square. We sit at the cement chess tables under the statue of Lenin lecturing the masses. Actually, it is a guy named Samuel Cox, a postman. We weep about the beauty of poetry, then fall off the benches laughing. Somehow we make it back up my stairs to block out the play, *The Cause of Gravity*, in the newsprint pad. Bob quickly draws a stage, which bleeds its magic through several pages.

All the pages are rippling like waves at the beach. We talk the play through. Me, I am a grounded sort, and Bob is all imagination. He creates new characters and songs and lickety-split we have the playbook. Bob knows many theater people. The 13th Street Repertory Theatre says *Yes*; Ray Gaspard says Yes; Bob's friend Francesca Barra says Yes; Donna Cohen says Yes. Of course, Bob and I and Rochelle are Yeses. We start rehearsals in Ray's loft on the Bowery. Bob directs. His concept of theater is very physical; if one needs a wheelbarrow on stage, two actors create it by one holding up the feet of the other. Rochelle and I are trained in theater games taught by my cousin Claire in Chicago. The play is magical and has evaporated, leaving no trace on the internet.

The play is a creation story with a lot of room for made-up mythology. I wear red tights and a ton of face makeup. I am a toy clown. I write the structure of the play and the poetic lines of dialogue, and Bob composes songs and dance numbers, adding pizzazz to the broader pallet. Eddie Waddell paints on fabric to make costumes that we pick up still wet. We hold them outside the window of the taxi roaring down to the 13th Street Theatre to dry on opening night.

The play is a touch of the marvelous. It makes sense on the poetic time horizon. Great forces of life collide with the hapless characters and objects; this conflict creates what we think of as gravity.

After the third and final performance, we have an all-night party at Ray's loft on the Bowery. We dance, stagger into the dawning light on the Bowery to find our various beds.

The success of this production is the fact of its production. It happened, so let's do it again.

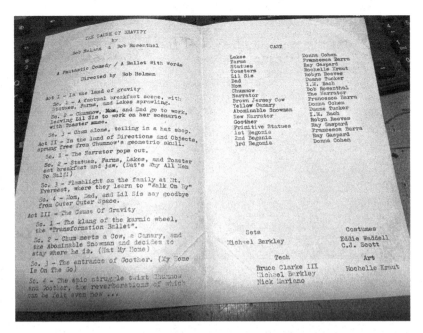

Late summer 1974, Bob Holman joins Rochelle and me at my grandfather's cottage on Lake Namakagon, northwest Wisconsin. We intend to write a play, drop acid, drink tequila. We wander over to the Namakagon Chief to down Leinenkugel beer and hamburgers. When we come out, the large dark sky over the lake is awash with the northern lights, dancing ribbons of crystal lights; we call them the Merry Prancers as we toddle back to the cottage.

Bob and I start hammering on my mother's 1930s manual Remington typewriter.

```
                DRAMATIS PERSONAE


          MABELLINE, The Whore of the Alpines
  The Duplegangers:

          BEN VENUTO  /  SLIK FECTOR

          LAMP  /  GINGER

          CHAIR  /  DUMPO

          CHIEF  /  SISSEL


Other Sundry Personae:

          VOICE

          CONDUCTOR

          TOWNSMEN

          CHIPMONK

          DUCKS

          TAPED VOICES, MAN & WOMAN
```

```
   Chief:     Away Fleas.
[Townsmen Scatter Mumbling Quacks.]

   Chief:     Whorry peaks!  She's here to sap my trees.  I must cut this off
              but how?  Quack quack buy her out then boat her ass down the
              craggy slopes.  Call in help!  I'll change my clothes.
              Or worse!  I must climb this peak and take a peek!

[Chief Off In Cloud Of Smoke, Red Lights Glare On.]


[Chief Storms Into Cottage, Flapping Shades, Lamp & Easy Chair.]
   Chief:     No one here.  But me.  Ha ha.  No whore fire baptising
              woman.  Nice decore.
  Chair & Lamp:  Thanks.
   Chief:     Beautiful interior design.
   Lamp:      Right.
   Chair:     Absolutly.
   Chief:     Tell me about her.
   Chair:     Her shape and weight is like a single musical note.
   Lamp:      Hair like morning's aurora and a voice that turns milk to
              Custard.
   Chair:     Ugh.
   Lamp:      Money?
   Chief:     Where?
   Chair:     The Alpine Miss, she from a city of people below the mountain
              ridges and in among a water sky, third form jazz, i ching,
              burning autos, reptiles, chipmonks, stripped bass,four
              stories up, one-way and no return, deposit, platform.
   Chief:     I can't get it.
   Lamp:      You should try Benny.
   Chair:     Ah, Benny!
   Chief:     Benny!  Benny who?
  Lamp & Chair:  Ben Venuto.
   Chair:     Tell him a bad road brings good people.
   Lamp:      I tell him of your improvement two track dirt patch, he'll
              get ya.  Send a note down with an avalanche and turn me out
              before you go.
```

Sample page of Alpine dialogue – everything comes to life.

We come up with the title *The Whore of the Alpines*. Somehow we manage to concoct the story of a young woman, perhaps a prostitute, who takes refuge high on an Alpine mountain. Bob and I write separately together, so a noir detective story parallels the main action. Each character plays dual roles. We incorporate the northern lights and litter the play with ducks calling out to each other.

We imagine that we are writing a feminist play. Mabelline is a strong character who knows what she wants and acts on it. In no way is she a victim of society. After we finish the play, we roll back to New York City and arrange to perform the play as a radio performance at the old WBAI studio in Midtown. It is performed live. David Herz is the narrator, and Didi Susan Dubelyew is Mabelline. Tom Carey is a chipmunk. It is fun and seems to come alive on the air. Bob and I give an interview to a female reporter; we talk it up as a feminist play. She doesn't argue. Another reviewer claims that we were setting back theater by decades.

Wasting no time, Bob and I plan our next masterpiece to welcome in the 200th anniversary of our nation's founding. The title is startlingly bold and memorable: *Bicentennial Suicide.* The Vietnam War has only just ended. New York City is in a financial crisis. The Daily News has a headline FORD TO

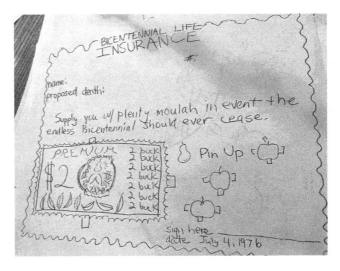

CITY DROP DEAD. Crack cocaine is littering our neighborhood with tiny vials. The country seems to be going nuts.

Our new play is ambitious. It will not only be a play but also a book, which we will distribute to the audience at the performance. We hand out Bicentennial Bucks with the program to "pay" for the book.

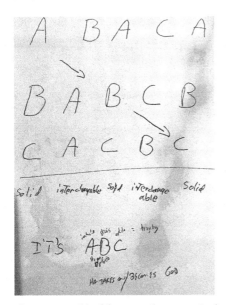

The acid trip for this play reveals an alternating structure for the contents. Hard and soft sections are to be repeated in a precise formulation. This allows Bob and I to write separately, then combine the sections. It also allows us to put extra poetry by Ted Berrigan and Alice Notley and the cast members into the book. I am still reading Yeats's *A Vision,* which influences the internal girding of the play.

Our basic story is the quest to get Uncle Sam to kill himself by falling for the oldest joke in the world, which is the serpent tricking Eve in the Garden of Eden. But our Uncle Sam is too obtuse and vain to fall for the joke. We have our usual assortment of animated objects. We also have a Yeats-like alternate world of floating characters including Uncle Sam and his consort, Columbia, the Gem of the Ocean. Bob Holman is Uncle Sam, and Rochelle is Columbia. I am the unearthly Ha, who is coupled with Mee Wee. We are prefiguring the creation of new pronouns to come in fifty years.

Appearing at

Soho Rep Theatre
19 Mercer, NYC
July 3, 4, 8, 9, 10

Hyde Park, NY
July 12, 13

Woodshole, Mass
July 15, 16, 17

St. Mark's Church
NYC
July 19

BICENTENNIAL SUICIDE
A Phenomenal Comedy / A Ballet w/ Words
BY

BOB HOLMAN & BOB ROSENTHAL

Directed by Bob Holman
Costumes by Eddie Waddell
assisted by Marion Farrier
Lights by Andrea Kirsch
Contrasting Director - Karen Cutler

Art by Rochelle Kraut

Photography by Barbara Baracks
Sets by Noh Art
Slide Projection by Lenny Neufeld
Box Office - Sam Davis
Book printed at St. Mark's Church
by Frontward Books

Cast in order of Appearance

BOB ROSENTHAL
Ha, Lenny Matisse Jamais

JO BRAHINSKY
MeeWee, Toaster, Ramona

KING BINGO
Uncle Sam, Radio, Dada Zen Cohen

KAREN CUTLER
Clock, Polly Tic, AppPear

SIMON SCHUCHAT
Table, Ahmid Pamoo, Milton Pressario

ROCHELLE KRAUT
Coffee Pot, Maize Midair
Columbia (Gem of the Ocean)

*Rochelle as Columbia
and Bob as Sam*

Simon Schuchat, me, Karen Cutler and Rochelle.

The mimeograph book is unique in mimeo technology in that it goes front to back and then flips over to go back to front; the first and last pages are back-to-back.

We open to small audiences in New York City. Who stays in town over the Fourth of July? The performances out of town have full audiences; we are well received.

1979 finds our next play. We want to adapt Ted Berrigan's *Clear the Range* to the stage. Ted wrote it by cutting up a Zane Gray Western novel. I do most of the editing from the book, and Bob shapes it into a play. Poets and friends: Steve Carey, Elinor Nauen, Tom Carey, Rachel Walling, Diane Thompson, Juan Valenzuela, Simon Pettet are in the cast. We produce it as part of a Poet's Theater festival at St. Clement's Church.

Simon, Rachel.

Bob and I are practiced at putting magic on stage, but now we are collaborating with Ted Berrigan's awesome sensibility. It is a marvelous production. Steve Carey is Cole Younger, who gets shot and falls backwards. I am behind him and always catch his head before it bangs the floor. Steve says, "There is somebody who saves my life every show."

Ted comes to the performance and loves it. Ted writes us:

> "Dear Bob. I annotated this [copy of the play] out of the shear pleasure and ecstasy of reading how beautiful a job it is – If any of my notes are of use fine –if not, I thought you might like it as a souvenir – love, Ted P.S. I can't stress enough how terrific a job I think you guys did making this version."

Elinor, Bob, Steve, Rachel.

Dogs: Rachel, Elinor, Bob, Juan.

Now the plays come easily. Bob is directing classic poets theater, such as Antonin Artaud's *Jet of Blood* and Tristan Tzara's *The Gas Heart*. Bob produces these at the Poetry Project. Rochelle does the art work. Bob's great facility is a never-say-die attitude. The *Jet of Blood* has a stage direction; "The Whore bites the hand of God." Impossible to imagine, but Bob knows how to do it. He has Rochelle make a giant blue paper hand concealing a red ribbon, which is carried onstage. Rochelle bites the wrist and grabs the ribbon with her teeth. She pulls it out doing a wild dance, trailing the red strip of blood through the space.

Rochelle, Simon

Young Man (Bob) and Whore (Rochelle) embrace in The Jet of Blood.

Bob Holman goes on to use Rochelle and Tom Carey again in *The Denby Plays* produced by the Eye & Ear Theater Company. 1982, poet friends, including Eileen Myles, organize a poets theater festival held at Charas Cultural Center. I direct the play *Australia* by Alice Notley. Michael Scholnick produces his own play *Providence*. I have no money to put into the play but I find a $20 bill in the street, which is just enough to make *Australia*. I get miffed at Simon Pettet because I feel he doesn't act fully in rehearsal. He says that he will at the performance. This is a poet waiting for the critical measure; the single performance is very good, and Simon does act strongly. Our three year old, Aliah, freaks out when he sees his mother on stage in 1982, in *The Denby Plays*.

I take him out to calm him. I don't do any more playwriting or acting for a while. Instead, I turn my arts organizing energy to teaming up with Simon Pettet to organize international poetry festivals.

Committee for International Poetry

Tom Pickard tells Simon and me that he is coming to New York and asks us to set up a poetry reading for him. Simon and I jump on this and ask Allen Ginsberg if we could organize this poetry reading and invite more British poets by using his nonprofit, The Committee on Poetry, Inc. He agrees, of course. We have a nice size audience. Allen Ginsberg comes to the readings. Simon and I arc off to a good start. We decide that we will make an art poster for each reading we organize.

Working for Allen naturally leads me to read poets from around the world. Allen meets them on his international tours and they gift him their books or have them sent.

Needless to say, the British poets write in English. With other festivals, we have to come up with a governing rule for translation. We decide that all poets will read their poems in their original language. A poem can only be fully understood if heard this way. Translations are to be read by American poets. The translations need only be prosaic in nature. The combination of the original with a literal translation works very well. America has no official language and although many languages are spoken, English is dominant. Our earliest goal is create a pan-national festival with poets from all over the globe, like those held at the Milkweg in Amsterdam. But there is no way to raise the necessary funding. The PEN American Center has limited resources but likes the idea. All public arts funding is restricted to only sponsoring American artists. We realize we have to make individual festivals and apply for support from parochial interests: Japan Society for Japanese poetry, Maison Française for French poetry, Festival of India for Indian poetry, etc. Organizing a festival of poetry has many moving parts. Simon and I are both overwhelmed. I keep an eye out for more people to help us. Marc Nasdor joins us and brings an incredible amount of energy and technical know-how, making our larger ambitions come true.

Poster by Malcolm Morley.

We get New York State readers funding and raise a cash contribution from the Guinness Corporation, which also supplies beer. We ask Josh Bear of the White Columns Gallery, and he agrees to provide the venue, April 30, and May 1, and 2, 1982. We have enough money to fly British poets in. Eric Mottram, one of Simon's old professors and a poet, agrees to participate. Simon and I approach the British painter Malcolm Morley to make a poster. When we visit Malcolm's Studio, he tells us that red and black are the best colors. He gives us an image; we make the poster using black with some red lettering. We have eight poets over the three days. We have a lot of Guinness stout and Harp lager. Tom Pickard is so impressed that he incorporates Guinness's name into one of his poems. The recording is played at a Guinness board meeting.

Poster by Bill Sullivan

Murat Nemet-Nejat comes to us proposing an evening of Turkish poets, which is presented at the Writer's Voice, at the West Side YMCA under the auspices of Jason Shinder. Murat stays with us to help with future events.

Poster by José Luis Cuevas.

At the Latin American Festival, Politics are impossible to avoid. The Puerto Rican poet Ivan Silen denounces us at the New York Public Library for being imperialist exploiters.

Poster by Sam Francis.

These are stellar readings by Japan's most revered poets and the most nonconformist poets. I am disappointed that we could not completely fill the Cooper Union's Great Hall.

POETS
FROM THE
PEOPLE'S
REPUBLIC
OF CHINA

Poster by Ai Wei Wei

Ai Wei Wei angrily yells at me because Reagan won the presidential election. We are driving to JFK in a cab to catch a plane to Los Angeles to meet the Chinese poets. The driver, a turbaned Sikh, is leaning back to hear me try to explain the complexity of the electoral college to Wei Wei. The first night in Los Angeles, my niece, Bryna, UCLA student, suggests we all go the Hamburger Haven restaurant. Jiang He orders chicken wings. The plate of wings is huge. He is embarrassed and accuses us of pulling a trick on him. He takes most of the wings back to the hotel. The poets eat those wings for next week. The poets make ceramic tiles at Woodland Pattern; Wei Wei draws me.

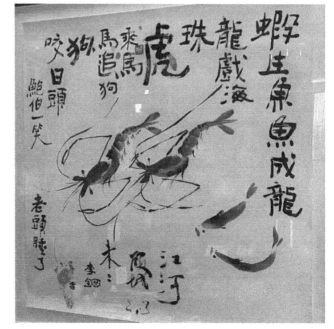

Li Gang brushes carp and shrimp, and the other poets write on a large sheet of watercolor paper. In the picture, the footprint is the child of Gu Cheng. Far left near the top is my name; it reads, "Bob laughs."

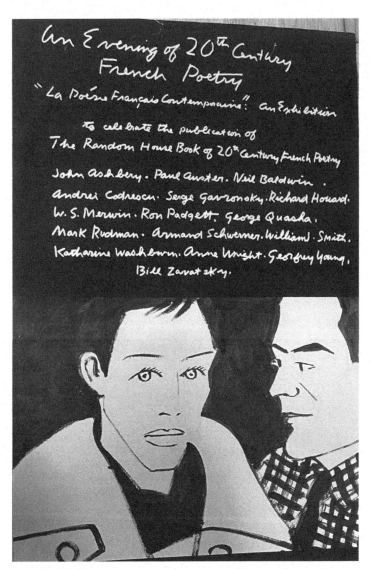

Poster by Alex Katz

An evening of French Poetry is a magical confluence of Paul Auster's *The Random House Book of Twentieth Century French Poetry* and a library exhibit on the same poets. The exhibit encompasses the Parish Hall of St. Mark's Church and many of the translators are there to read.

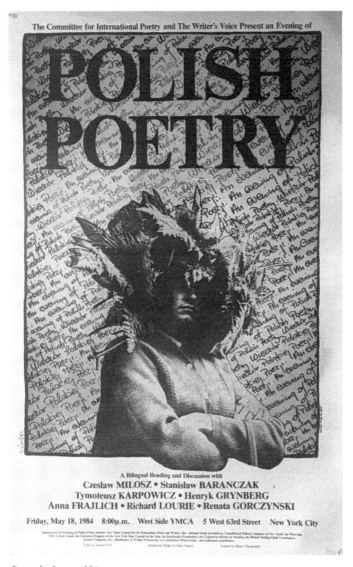

The Committee for International Poetry and The Writer's Voice Present an Evening of

POLISH POETRY

A Bilingual Reading and Discussion with

**Czeslaw MILOSZ • Stanislaw BARANCZAK
Tymoteusz KARPOWICZ • Henryk GRYNBERG
Anna FRAJLICH • Richard LOURIE • Renata GORCZYNSKI**

Friday, May 18, 1984   8:00p.m.   West Side YMCA   5 West 63rd Street   New York City

Poster by Joanna Voit

Once again Jason Shinder hosts us at the West Side Y. Poetry is the most beautiful oral aspect of any language. I always feel that Polish sounds harsh, as it is screamed at me by my Polish landlords on East 12th Street. Later, when we organize Polish poets, the mellifluous sounds of Adam Zagajewski reading his poems in Polish is breathtakingly beautiful.

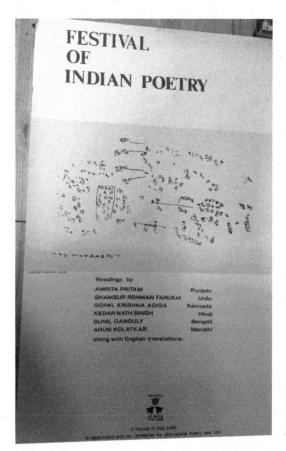

The poster shows "magic script" which is Indian Tribal artwork imitating Hindi script at the Bharat Bhavan, Bhopal.

Kabali warns us he would picket the Indian Readings at Museum of Modern Art because we are not planning to include a Tamil poet. So we invite the great Tamil poet and translator A.K. Ramanujan from the University of Chicago, and have Kabali read the English for him. After the readings, Kabali invites us to his apartment. He prepares a great Southern Indian feast.

When the Indian poets are in Santa Fe, New Mexico, a generous India hand makes a fine Indian meal. It is laid out on the floor. There is no silverware. Ashok Vaijpai notices our Western looks of concern. Ashok calls out loudly, "What, no silverware!" Arun Kolatkar confides to me that he wants to covertly eat some beef on the trip. We decide to treat him to Steak and Eggs in Boulder, Colorado, which serves organic beef. Kedar Nath Singh asks me what to order at breakfast; I suggest French toast. He is skeptical but orders it. We put Maple syrup on it, which he has never tasted before. He loves it. Gopla Kishna Adiga, a Marathi Brahman poet, and his wife walk up and down a whole isle of bread at a supermarket in Santa Fe. They check all the breads and buy the whitest and purest bread – *Wonder Bread.*

Poster by Rudy Burckhardt

    Our festival of English speaking Caribbean poets overfills the auditorium at the Brooklyn Museum as Louise Bennett holds everybody captive with her poems. Andrew Beddoe speaks an arcane pirate patois that is chilling.

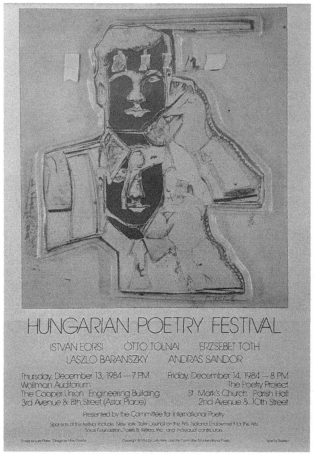

Poster by Larry Rivers

Istvan Eorsi is an old friend and translator of Allen's. He is a well-known playwright who suffered in Hungarian jails, 1958.

There is a tremendous amount of work represented by these posters. Not the posters themselves, rather the festivals they announce. Each one needs fundraising, preparation for bilingual readings by creating translations, transportation, food and housing, entertainment, and documentation. Marc makes sure all the readings are recorded. He creates a radio program, *Poetry International*, using Barbara Barg as its announcer; this creates the pan-national festivals we always yearn for. Marc includes poets from all the festivals.

For the actual festivals, we use well-known venues: St Mark's Church, the Cooper Union; the Museum of Modern Art; the CUNY Graduate Center; the New York Public Library; the West Side YMCA; White Columns; the Brooklyn Museum; Woodland Pattern in Milwaukee; UCLA, Santa Fe Arts Center; the University of Colorado in Boulder. The Indian poets and the Chinese poets traveled on national tours with us.

We rely on our native naivete to help program poets from the same country that don't like one another. Anne Waldman and I were invited by the Festival of India to hear Indian poets in Bhopal, India. The festival was organized according to Allen Ginsberg's suggestions; it included tribal dancers, Vedic chanters, bohemian poets, and Namdeo Dhasal, a Dalit (untouchable caste) poet. When Vedic chanters went on too long, the organizers turned to Anne and me and said, "See, he goes on and on." The festival was designed to show us how unworkable some of Allen's ideas would be. We fail to convince the Indian government to bring Namdeo Dhasal. But in New York we do mix in the English-writing Mumbai poet Nissim Ezekiel who is Jewish. The other Indian poets tolerate it. We mix political enemies at the Latino American festival. We know Li Gang is a watchdog for the powerful China Writers Association. He turns out to be an affable guy and not a problem.

Our audiences are often from the New York City communities of the poets we featured. Our own friends do not come out so often. I ask my friend Eileen Myles if she would come to the Japanese poets reading at the Cooper Union; she replies that she does not need to know what the poets of Japan are doing. Eileen is not anti-Asian. She is enjoying a natural height in the literary world in New York and doesn't see her need to hear these poets. Simon, Marc, Murat and I do feel the need, and we benefit ourselves from translating, meeting, and presenting poets from around the world so we do not need the full approbation of our peers. The amount of time it takes to organize and stage these events and the lack of remuneration start to become an issue in my poor household with two small kids. I promise Rochelle that I will stop doing festivals.

Frontward Books – Mimeography

1974; Rochelle and I decide to start a new mimeo press in New York City. We call it Frontward Books. We use the mimeo machine in the Poetry Project office. Neil Hackman is publishing *Out There*. Michael Scholnick, Greg Masters, and Gary Lenhart publish *Mag City*; Simon Schuchat publishes *432 Review*, which is legal size. Rochelle makes covers for *Out There* and *432 Review*. She also makes the cover for our first poetry book, *A Feeling For Leaving* by Ted Berrigan. I feel blessed to be typing up the raw manuscript. I work hard with a great pleasure laying out one of Ted's signature poems for the first time, "So Going Around Cities."

Rochelle's cover is hand-colored with oil pastel crayons.

Frontward Books publish Alice, ourselves, as well as Neil Hackman before he changes his name to Ravi Singh. Art Lange creates a book in which each poem uses a title of a Thelonious Monk composition. Susie Timmons book is made of early works; when I try to talk to her about a poem, she snatches it out of the pile. So I shut up, not wanting to make the manuscript smaller. We publish Danny Krakauer's first book of poetry. He is in his seventies; I read decades of his poetry, from the 1950s to the present. In the end, I pick the poems Danny writes for Alice's workshop; Alice makes the cover for Danny.

My first poetry teacher, Steve Toth, creates a book based on the Kabbalah. We publish early Ed Friedman journals. We become skilled at mimeography; start to print our books double-sided. There is so much mimeographing going on that we hold collating parties in the Parish Hall of St. Mark's church. While walking around tables set out with the pages we gossip and collate and walk out with new reading material.

We also combine to mail out the books. We called it Packet Poets. Book rate is 89 cents for the first pound and 29 cents subsequently. We all had the same mailing list, so we all saved money by making each packet heavier. The whole idea is to give the books away. Bob Wilson at the Phoenix Bookshop takes seven copies of a new handmade book as he has seven libraries with a standing order for them. We aren't getting published by big presses and need to make our own works a reality. When the postal rates jump precipitously, it ends our publication efforts.

The other publication fun we communally have is mimeographing our scandal sheet called *Caveman*. Alice Notley, Eileen Myles, Simon Schuchat, Rochelle Kraut, Susie Timmons, Elinor Nauen, and I start the magazine. Simon leaves town soon but we continue to ascribe our magazine to him. Alice Notley writes her memories to me, "Do you remember when you invented the second version of Caveman pretending to be Simon Schuchat and you and I did the first issue together? And Ted being annoyed at not being invited said after we'd done it that we didn't know how and invited Eileen to do the second issue with him. After a couple more issues he said what it took to do it was the Crazy Women and Bob Rosenthal. (Of course, he had become essential too.)"

The rules for Caveman are 1. We must cut the stencil in real time together and 2. There is no going back to rewrite. We have pieces of writing by Ted and Alice but don't always put their names on them. We erroneously ascribe most of the material. The last issue is dated to the closest holiday, July 4, 1983. In it Ted quips, "Lorna Smedman: How could somebody so round be so square?" Ted dies on July 4, 1983. Suddenly a generation of poets grows up. Some of us put down our childish pleasures and raise children instead. Lorna is furious with me and Rochelle and all for this Cavemen quip. We explain that Ted wrote it, but he is gone and Lorna stays mad until we are in a car returning from lawn party at Murat's home in Westchester. I am too drunk and suddenly have to heave; by the time the car pulls over, I have upchucked a little on Lorna. She becomes nice to me again. It goes to show that anger is impossible to actually figure out.

Writing collaborations is a way to be social, especially before the private portals of computers inhabit our lives. We set a typewriter up on a hassock with a blank piece of paper in the living room. Have a party while we take turns typing a poem. Generally, we do not look at the preceding lines. Three or four pages fall out of the machine. Usually, these group efforts are not memorable, but they are fun party games. 1977; a crew of poet friends, Michael Scholnick, Susie Timmons, David Herz, Simon Schuchat and I are hammering out a collab at my apartment. Hendrix is on the record player; it is a stifling summer night. Suddenly Jimi's extended notes bend more than usual and the lights dim and then go out. The city is plunged into total darkness. Rochelle is out on Second Avenue, and expected home. We troop out into the blackness, and walk down the avenue until we find her. Excitedly, we buy more beer and go back to write by candlelight. We go up to roof, and look east, where the skies over Brooklyn are littered with police helicopters shining searchlights down on neighborhoods where looting is happening. The stars appear overhead. We have never seen them so close before on the Lower East Side.

June 13, 1977

CAVEMANCAVEMANCAVEMANCAVEMANCAVEMANCAVEMANCAVEMANCAVEMANCAVEMANCAVEMANCA
VEMANCAVEMANCAVEMANCAVEMANCAVEMANCAVEMANCAVEMANCAVEMANCAVEMANCAVEMANCAVE

I.

"To the foot of every work of art is chained this cannonball that holds down the soul after death."

    --Larry Fagin

JOHN ASHBERY: THE WORKING MAN'S POET

Stepping out from the Young Marxist Ladies Working League meeting last Wednesday night I wantonly strolled into a small bourgeois bookstore containing a wide variety of neo-decadent products by writing workers...it was there I stumbled onto this gem of prole doggerel, something to work by, something to rattle in the sweaty workers weary head while he/she gives his/her blood and sweat to the Kapitalist machine... I dwell too long on my counter-productive individual experience: let's look at the text of this Wunderkind of the Common Man/Woman: John Ashbery. The devious title alone was indicative of the political machinations of Comrade Ash-Berry's "mind," The Double Dream of Spring. The implications are obvious: "double dream," the continual strife, the divergent visions of the workers and the foul money mongers, and Spring, the landed deity of change, revolution is constant as is the drear workers condition.

See this quote from this daring revolutionary ditty, An Outing: "These things....that you are going to have- are you paid specially for them?"   The implications are obvious. Or see The Hod Carrier. Or again, let the title speak for itself. Truly sublime, truly a paean to the worker who does carry "hod."

I could go on, but just to get to basics, the words "Worker," "labor," "conditions" and of course, the decadent term "vacation" are reiterated scores of times. A worker can pick it up over a brief break, get a quick shot of revolutionary ardor....We thank you poet of the working man, John Ashberrry. You are a true word-worker.

    --Eileen Myles

Special To Caveman

SHE DOES get nervous from time to time, haunted by that cold January morning when her 56-year-old husband, Casey, kept shouting "Fire...get out...get out," and she looked for his artificial leg and couldn't find it.

Before Going Out

I smooched you pretty lightly
As you slept. Of your precious rest
Precious you were not bereft, or budged
From it. I watched you dreaming, and
Saw the dream modified, though reasonably;
So it seemed you should be left to lie. And lying
There, beside, I should watch. To make sure
Provocateurs wouldn't botch your fluttering eye
Henna'd hair vision. Dream, I've gone
To work. So Dream, be safe, and
Don't let up till later. But
Get up, go, when I careen home
In a clapping Double R, and stop me
Coming through the door - You!
With a smack right on my kisser

    -- Steve Levine

CAVEMANCAVEMANCAVEMANCAVEMANCAVEMANCAVEMANCAVEMANCAVEMANCAVEMANCAVEMANCAV
CAVEMANCAVEMANCAVEMANCAVEMANCAVEMANCAVEMANCAVEMANCAVEMANCAVEMANCAVEMANCAVEMA

JANUARY TUESDAY 30, 1979
CAVEMANCAVEMANCAVEMANCAVEMANCAVEMANCAVEMANCAVEMANCAVEMANCAVEMANCAVEM
ANCAVEMANCAVEMANCAVEMANCAVEMANCAVEMANCAVEMANCAVEMANCAVEMANCAVEMCVEMA

IV

"BUT YOU'RE LOOKING AT THE ACTUAL GIRL! DOES SHE <u>LOOK</u> SHORT TO YOU??"
I said, "She's standing next to her hairdresser and her hairdresser's
short too, so you can't tell."

— Andy Warhol'; '70 ·uh 5

TO OUR READERS:

I respectfully dedicate this issue of <u>Caveman</u> to my growth and develop-
ment as a poet and personal person.
The Editors

DIFFICULTIES

Uncle Palamede, please tell me what I can do
     about this web I keep spinning out of lies.
I gave up submission, I have a weak will
     but I notice the nun's life is very hard.
So I took up some of my habit's hem, and now I notice
     I still arrange it elegantly over my shoulder.
Then I withdrew into myself my dear Palamede
     and now I notice that I am arranging my life, constantly.
I gave up discipline, and now I notice
     that I am in chains all day.
I worked hard at dissolving my ego,
     and now I am proud of myself.
When the mind wishes to do battle with the passions,
     still it will hold on to one last teardrop.
Kabir says, Listen oh my little one,
     Damn few foxes fuck better than you.

Helena Hughes

SEVEN BRIDES FOR SEVEN BROTHERS

It's too cold today. What do you mean? it's fucking wonderful
today! Fuck. What are you a fucking Indian? Do only
Indians fuck? Only Indians say Ugh after they fuck. I
said Fuck not Ugh. Ugh.
Alice Notley

CAVEMANCAVEGIRLCAVEBOYCAVEMANCAVEMANCAVEMANCAVEMANCAVEMANCAVEMANNERS
CAVEMANCAVEMANCAVEGRANDPACAVECHINAMANCAVEMANCAVEMANCAVEGIRLCAVE

CAVEMAN CAVEMANCAVEMANCAVEMANCAVEMANCAVEMANCAVEMANCAVEMANCAVEMANCAVEMANCAV
EMANCAVEMANCAVEMANCAVEMANCAVEMANCAVEMANCAVEMANCAVEMANCAVEMANCAVEMANCAVEMANC

M   "Take this meat from my forehead. mI can't use it anymore"

"Give it to Bob"

m   "Do you think I'm pretty."

EDITORIAL

CAVEMAN – the Magazine of humor and REVENGE. Dedicated to the concept that
everything is so Silly. We make everyone, good and bad, look bad. CAVE
MAN is dedicated to the concept of truth in all it's roots, delving beyond
and below ACULTURE to get to the root, the essence, the base of the CAVE
MAN in us all. That is why I'm most qualified to edit this Anniversary
issue, the FIRST 100 YEARS. Though I am not a part of this everyday local
scene, I, through my embodiment of this essence of Caveman, which is
INSTINCT, by my instinctual knowledge of what is happening, even though I'm
so far away, buried in the gilded halls of learning, even though I know
nothing, somehow I got it all down.   — Simon Schuchat
                                                Gang of One

CAVEMAN — THE FIRST HUNDRED YEARS

100th ANNIVERSAY ISSUE

July 4, 1983   # 10^2

L*A*M*E*N*T   For the First 100 Years of Caveman

So much has changed when first we turned our furrowed brow to publication.
Before the firey flames of destiny tore sonorously into our lives and
equipáge, before our editor Simon Schuchat was lost to a foreign power and
then the throes of academe, remember when we would join hands in making
magic, publication at it's purest Mimeo! which would stain our fingertips
in earnest, eyeballs too,,tow the people are mild, indolent, timid and
superstitious. We wave across the empty halls of knowledte from our vain to
towers of fame. Even sex has fallen away! Comradely bodies with their
surreal code of drunken poetics have given way to grant-seeking, slave
keeping, bestiality and death cults. One soul hardly now knows another.
We who remember spot on the civil wars, the flesh-eating, compugraphics,
type-setting and butt-hole. Caveman got down, grunting and feeling, a
poem by marc nasdor was considered worth it.

WHERE ARE THEY NOW

Sara Miles	Olson Macintytre	Richard BAndanza
RAgina Beck	Charles North	Brad Gooch
Anne Waldman	Lee Sherry	Helena Hughes
Michael Scholnick	Diane Thompson	Yuki Hartman
Michael Summers	Karen Cutler	Pat Jones
Michael Slater	Libby Howse	Vicki Hudspith
Maggie Dubris	Patti Landi	Sam Shepard
Bill Zavatsky	Annabel Levitt	Patti Smith
Billy McKay	John Yaua	Belle Starr
Barbara Baracks	FT Prince	Janet Hamill
Kathy Acker	Gary Lenhart	Steven Hall
Barbara BArg	Nikki Giovanni	Maria Mancini
Tom Carey	Helen Adam	Will Bennet
Lincoln Sales	Bernadette Mayer*	Susie Timmons
Kevin Clarke	Joel Lewis	Harris Schiff
Bernard Whitelaw Alphabet		Ed Friedman
Antler	Jimmy Schuyler	Harry Barnes
Nina Zavancovich	Bill Berkson	Margo Howard-Howard
Jim Carroll	Greg Masters	Ted Greenwald
Ted Berrigan	Libby Notley	David Herz
Didi Susan Dubelyew	Michael Lally	Sibyl
Mark Breeding	Ann Rower	Lita Hornick
Larry Rivers	John Fisk	Madeline Keller
Fanny Howe	Susan Howe	Maureen Owen
Charles Walsh	Maria Gitten / David Franks	Charlie Vermont
Bernie Welt		POEZ

Life & Death

We party after poetry readings or on holidays. Ed lives in a narrow loft in Soho; Rochelle and Ed make endless potato latkes for a huge crowd on Hanukah. I remember grating potatoes until my fingertips are bloody. Helena Hughes makes dinner parties, as does Susan Cataldo.

Lita Hornick hosts an annual poets party in her Fifth Avenue apartment. There is a buffet supper and musicians and, of course, liquor. It is an easy party to crash. We would go in as older poets no longer partying as hard and soon get our own invites. Lita also takes poets to dinner at expensive French restaurants on 57th street. She always says, 'Order what you like; there are no prices on the menu." Lita is the founder of *Kulchur* magazine and has been a patron of the arts for decades. Rochelle and I become part of the stable of poets she regularly takes to dinner. Her husband, Morty, never comes out with us. We learn to eat fast if we want dessert. Lita has a habit of suddenly announcing that we are leaving, even if you are still savoring your meal. We have drinks and amuse Lita as best we can. Allen Ginsberg takes this photo in Lita's apartment.

No one dies innocent, meaning *knowing nothing.* Death is a teacher. The first sudden death in our crew of poets is Michael Scholnick. Michael is everyone's closest friend. His personal sense of grammar makes him inexplicable to many people, and so he is a safe repository for sharing intimacies. I find that when we have a conversation Michael pauses so long in his sentences that I tend to jump in and interrupt. I decide to record him talking to figure out what is going on. I tape an interview; as I transcribe the tape,

Lita Hornick in her dining room, dessert for our lunch, Richard Bosman's "The Norseman" on her north wall, we thought to buy Franz Kline exhibit at Whitney Museum of a few blocks from her Park Avenue apartment. Writer, critic, excellent art & poetry Patron. February 2, 1995. — Allen Ginsberg

Michael's sentences come out pithy and clear. They are long and take twisty turns, which he ponders in his head before he returns to the sentence. He always lands on his feet no matter how long the pause. The sentence is a sentence.

Michael dies of a sudden heart stop in his mother's apartment with his wife, Nelly, and two-year-old daughter, Beth, while celebrating his mother's birthday. He dies as if there is an end date stamped on his heart. We, the grieving, are suddenly older and not wiser.

Despite Ted Berrigan's death being quietly anticipated; it made a profound ripple in the poetry fabric of the Lower East Side. Ted died of a ruptured liver in 1983. Ted, Jack Kerouac, and Chogyam Rinpoche all die the same death at the same age, 47. Ted is a hero in my life. I and many other young poets model Ted's education, lifestyle of dedicated writing, and barbed acuity. We move to New York because of Ted. Ted recommends me to Allen Ginsberg. Ted tells me after a prose reading of mine, "Oh you Jews!" A compliment indeed. The community is breaking up before Ted's death. Bernadette and Lewis fight with Ted and Alice. It is so hard to be around parents divorcing. The craziness is really about Ted dying, and none of us can see it. Our time isn't over it; it has a new name. People move away, have children, get new jobs. Our extended childhood is over.

Susan Cataldo is a close friend. She is a terrific poet. Susan and I go to Weight Watchers together. She is an old hand. Drinking water is part of weight loss. Susan tells me not to worry about getting up at night to pee, "It means you're properly hydrated." I still remember that as I often get up in the night. Susan provides an Italian Christmas dinner with lasagna; all the guests are Jewish.

Susan becomes ill with ovarian cancer. When she lies in the hospice hospital near the end of her hardships, she is unsettled, thrashing and not able to talk. When I visit, I bring a Frank O'Hara book and read his poetry to her. She settles down and breathes regularly and slowly. Her friends are impressed. I leave the volume for the reading of more poetry. But it does not work as well. Reading poetry is about adding a poet's voice to the poem, any poem.

Rochelle writes up a tribute to Susan for the Poetry Project Newsletter.

Susan Cataldo September 15, 1952 – April 25, 2001

Susan Cataldo was born in the Bronx. Growing up with some hard knocks, she ran away to the East Village in 1968. She eventually worked for Children's Meeting, one of the early daycare centers in the neighborhood, while raising her son, Kris.

In 1978, her friend and neighbor, poet Susie Timmons, introduced her to the Poetry Project, where she took part in poetry workshops led by Ted Berrigan, Alice Notley, and Harris Schiff, who became her mentors. Sensitive and warm with a fierce intelligence, wicked wit, and exuberant humor, she wrote with authority, had a keen aesthetic ear and eye, and took artistic and emotional risks.

In the 1990s, she returned to college and graduated from Hunter College with honors in psychology. Throughout, she continued to write and work on several manuscripts. Attending a prestigious graduate program in biopsychology at SUNY Binghamton, her studies were interrupted in 1998 by the discovery that she had ovarian cancer. With the help of chemotherapy, alternative medicine, the programs at Gilda's Club New York, and the loving support of her many friends, her husband, and family, she faced her illness, as she faced her life, with honesty and courage. With love, humor, and openness, she continued to nourish her creative spirit and those around her until her last day.

Danny is dying. He has an enlarged spleen. His doctors cannot give a fatal prognosis, so Danny cannot get palliative hospice care. I look in on Danny and shop for him. John Godfrey, who is a nurse, visits Danny and rubs his skin with emollients. Meals on Wheels calls to tell me Danny has not taken in the previous day's meal. I trepidatiously approach the apartment and let myself in. Danny is dead on his bed. He has taken all his meds and feebly cut his wrist. A trickle of old blood drips down his arm. I look at Danny for a while and pray for him to have an easy path forward. I call 911. When the police come, they are not interested in me. It becomes a crime scene. I am literally pushed out the door, and the yellow tape goes up.

Danny's landlord is the photographer Timothy Greenfield Sanders. Danny had ceded the contents of his apartment to the New York City attorney general who cedes it to the landlord. His only family is a sister, Hannah, who lives in Israel. I want to rescue some of Danny's books and also retrieve the stash of cash he hid among the first editions. I make a deal with Timothy. Somehow, I can't remember how, I make it easy for him to takeover Danny's 212 area code landline, which is so old that it carries special low rates. I agree to do this if I can enter the apartment and take out Danny's writing manuscripts and some of his poetry collection. I find the cash, which is enough to buy Danny a grave and a marker. My rabbi holds a service for Danny. There is enough money left over to send to Hannah. There is also a City Lights first-edition *Howl* with the tipped-in cover and a first-edition Ace-double *Junkie*.

The night before Danny's burial, I dream that I am in the middle of a long line of people who all know Danny; we are walking into a hole in the ground. I realize that Danny stays alive as long as there is one person who remembers him or knows about him left aboveground.

Jim Brodey lives on all the edges in life; at times he is homeless, crack addicted; his life as a poet is much brighter than its hard ending. Jim contracts AIDS, moves to California, cleans up, and lives out his remaining time in hospice helping others as he himself perishes. His poems are collected from magazines, books, friends; they live in history and in the hearts of those who follow the history of poetry. What more is there? Eternal life?

Steve Carey dies in bed. Like Ted, he lies on his bed for a couple years. We visit and talk of friends living and dead. His poetry is collected in a handsome book. When we die, we get the book that we didn't see in our own lifetime. It is a book edited by friends who only want the very best for the gone poet. It is better than an epigram on a tombstone but more ephemeral.

The Boys Dorm

Rochelle and I move into 437 East 12th Street in 1974. We take Rebecca Wright's apartment and buy her furniture. Rebecca leaves me all of her Allen Ginsberg books, as she no longer needs them. I read Ginsberg in a serious way for the first time. John Godfrey lives on the top floor. Larry Fagin lives one flight up from us and in the back. He likes to visit us at dinnertime. We invite him to sup. One day he exposes his penis to Rochelle who is indignant, points at him and tells him, "Shame on you!" We don't invite Larry in anymore. Richard Hell lives in the back. In a couple of years the entire Mag City crew moves in: Greg Masters, Michael Scholnick, Gary Lenart. Elinor Nauen starts to call 437 the Boy's Dorm. She says the girls will not date these guys because they will just go home and gossip. Simon Pettet moves in. Steve Levine moves in. Arthur Russell lives here. Cliff Fyman moves in. Lorna Smedman moves in. We are friends with Joanne

© *Stephan Shames, 1982 for People Magazine.*

In front of 437 East 12th Street. Left to right: Edith Ginsberg, Allen's stepmother; Cliff Fyman; Bob Rosenthal; Allen Ginsberg; John Godfrey; Steven Taylor; Peter Orlovsky; Greg Masters; Michael Scholnick.

Brahinsky and her daughter Anna, who live upstairs. We mimeo a building newsletter called *The 12th Street Rag*, a once very popular ragtime number. We put in recipes and silly poems. It's a precursor to *Caveman*.

Jim Brodey lives here for a while. He edits a giant anthology of poetry by poets who either live at, or have lived at, or stayed a short while at 437. The book fattens up nicely, but no one publishes it and the copy is lost.

Rochelle and I get involved in the rent strike against the landlords, a strange old couple who eventually also move into the building. They gave the tenants hot water for one hour in the morning and one hour in the evening. They line their windows with newspapers. We go on rent strike and all heat and hot water stops. The judge in our case is suddenly changed and the new judge says that we have to actually put our saved-up rent into a court-sealed bank account. Rochelle and I decide to move out rather than pay in. We move to East 11th Street in 1977. This is about the last year for inexpensive apartment rentals.

Allen Ginsberg and Peter Orlovsky move in just before Rochelle and I leave. Soon I am working for him and coming back to the building five days a week. The landlady mutters in Polish as I walk up the stairs, but gradually she stops even coming out of her door. I still help on the rent strike as Allen Ginsberg's representative.

Rene Ricard moves in. He is crazed on crack. He wants me to go up to the roof with him. I do. Then he goes to the airshaft and points into the Blasco's sixth floor apartment. Rene says to me that they are killing people in there. "Come look." I am afraid to get too close to the edge of the airshaft; I fear Rene pushing me over. I instead turn and run back to Allen's apartment.

My association with 437 ends when we move Allen's office to Union Square. I can't work around Peter Orlovsky after he assaults me, 1984.

The 11th street apartment is big but it is highly flawed. We have two kids sleeping in the back in bunk beds, and Rochelle and I sleep in the middle room, which has a bathtub in it. The kitchen is big enough to accommodate a table. I have a writing desk in the front room where there is a good view of the Empire State Building. There are no doors to the rooms; the apartment is a continuous floor through. Exhaust fumes leak into the kids' room. The whole building is infested with roaches and mice. We are rent stabilized but don't want to live there with no privacy as the boys get to be teens. Rochelle and I look for ways to move within the East Village. Rents have skyrocketed and we cannot afford any move. I start my next mission impossible in 1987: urban homesteading. At least this all-consuming project will benefit my entire family, not just me.

We research urban homesteading and apply at the Habitat for Humanity building being renovated on East 6th Street. Rochelle and I are rejected because we are not racially diverse. They do accept a bunch people who are diverse but are also dealing drugs in Tompkins Square. We need to avoid social workers to get into homesteading. At Children's Liberation Daycare in P.S. 122, we become acquainted with the 367 East 10th Street Homesteaders. We join them. In 1994, after seven years of weekly physical toil and epic battles with bureaucrats, we get our Certificate of Occupancy. Rochelle and I move into a three-bedroom duplex apartment. This poem is an operatic version of our physical struggle:

URBAN HOMESTEADING

Homesteading is melancholy like a Rachmaninoff concerto
It opens with the soft notes of donning hard hats and gloves
whispers through masks that ease steam under eyeglasses
the opening theme gathers the tools and distributes the tasks
final cups of coffee and thoughts of friends idling in bed Sat. morn
trudge the aging rusted tread pull down the ceiling
jam it crack it with a crowbar then insert a long board
and pull down the crackling lathing plaster dust and eighty years of dirt
flies down around your ears
Yes remember that theme?
repeat till all the plaster and lathing and wood are down
pick out the lathing shovel up the plaster bucket it down

smash, pull, bend break walls bucket them down
the cadenza is buckets of rubble on the pulley lowering
             gloves slightly burning
floor after floor week after week horsehair flies up the nose
eyes water, back aches what fun everyone is sexy as
                        a sack of Idahos
AH a recitative, a glass of water, shuffle off to lunch
                        get whistled at by women lunching Life Cafe
meet with the city meet with the state meet with each other
sell hot dogs throw a dance talk to bank make the second movement
                                      balance
cut pipes, cut wires, cut fingers eat lead paint tamper with asbestos
ARGH! Will I ever play the piano again?
the dumpsters come and go, come and go
the building spills its guts
and the bureaucrats make you wait, the conductor's baton must be certified
the wait to rebuild continues and no one says why
the housing shortage continues and no one speeds the process to rehab.
the great Russian winter is just beginning
come on, tune up your long johns and keep in the struggle
one B-1 bomber is worth forty-five hundred buildings rehabilitated
that means 180,000 people housed
that's just a clue you've heard the music you know the score

1989

This life as an artist apart from general society is what enables me to work for the great bard Allen Ginsberg. In my own neighborhood, I am not Ginsberg's secretary; I am my own poet self. I intersect with Allen, but I am not one of those he praises. I do not show Allen my poetry. I avoid feelings of jealousy as he promotes other poets. I have a Leo's pride in my own accomplishments. This also makes it possible to be with Allen for so long without a nagging feeling of disappearing into his woodwork. I think it makes Allen respect me as both an inside agent and an outside agent. He appreciates the international readings; he allows me to spend office time on my homesteading work. He seeks me out for advice on housing. Allen accepts me as a poet; he knows me to be a poet. I have no need to prove it to him. At the end of his life, when I tell him that I will write about him, he takes my hand and sends me energy. When I say to him that it will be like *Cleaning Up New York*, his pleasure is increased. In *Straight Around Allen*, I begin each chapter with my poetry. Not to rub it in, but to establish a dramatic irony. The reader will know my poetry better than Allen ever does. Existence encompasses all manner of levels. My life as a poet continues to make me whole in the thin air we daily breathe.

2006 – 2016

Heschel High

After a decade of floating ignorantly through religious services, I up my practice. Elinor Nauen tells me about the morning service in 2004. She says it is fast, and informal in that you worship together but don't have to be friends. I start to make it to the 7 a.m. minyan. I soon get curious about tefillin; Steve Jacobson teaches me how to wrap my first set. The first time I ever wear tefillin, I have a vision afterward on First Avenue. I see the sky unzip itself and reveal more sky. Elinor now chides me to become an adult bar mitzvah. On the 4th of Elul, my fifty-fourth Jewish birthday, I become a bar mitzvah for real! My parashah is "Shoftim," that, among other things, offers advice about prophets. A true prophet is one whose prophecy comes true. I draw Ginsberg into my d'var:

> Ginsberg never claimed to be an agent of a holy voice. He was a human voice of candor. As the ancient prophets did, he placed his messages in the language of the common person. We read the prophets for they are not mysterious. They paid the human price of their gift and burden. We honor them by chanting and contemplating the comfort and the challenge they still provide. For us, the first step of teshuvah is the bravest. Unripe dreams are within us all; the voices of prophets are on the street waiting to be heard. Our rabbis say: Ever since the Temple was destroyed, prophecy was taken from the prophets and given to fools and children.

*

I am part fool and part child. I am the schlub in the back and these are my words:

We are on the road to Zion, but there is no road
We are praying for directions but hear only our own voices
We suffer faults and the chains that bind us to them
Yet footfalls follow footfalls through the echoing night
The smallest match struck in the darkness
is a mighty illumination
So bright we must cover our eyes as with the Sh'ma

Listen for daybreak's blasts
There is so much behind you
There is no reason not to go on – to the summit
You will find a part of you already there
Patiently waiting to see your face

A new Jewish thought occurs to me; I should teach in a Jewish setting. My friend
Ethan and I head for the schnapps after services. I tell him that I am looking for a
full-time teaching job. I add that I want it to be at a Jewish school so I will get the
Jewish holidays off. He tells me that his son's English teacher at Heschel High just got
fired. On Monday, I write to the head of school whose name I find on the Heschel
website. No answer comes. I remember that my rabbi's children go to Heschel and ask
Rabbi Sebert to recommend me. He writes a sweet note to the head of the high school
division. He says I am an "interesting fellow;" I do secure an invitation to apply for the
vacant position. Heschel is a first name school; Ahuva, the head of the high school, asks
me to meet with her. I know that my decades working for Allen Ginsberg will either
help me or sink me in her eyes. Heschel is a progressive school, which values the arts.
I speak with Ahuva in her sixth-floor office, sunlight streaming in behind her. I feel
super-relaxed. Where does this confidence come from? I am usually a nervous wreck. I
lean back in my chair and cross my legs, talk about the adjunct teaching I am doing at
CUNY. I also talk a little about Allen and discover that she likes poetry; in fact, she is a
scholar of the medieval Jewish Spanish poets, like Judah Halevi. Ginsberg is not going to
hurt me here.

Ahuva asks me to do a model lesson for the tenth grade. I prepare a lesson on
William Blake's *Songs of Innocence* and *Songs of Experience*. I want to compare and
contrast the poems whose titles appear in both *Innocence* and *Experience*. As I walk
from Columbus Circle down 60th Street to the school, I think, "Here is a learning
experience. No matter if I get the job, the practice of doing a model lesson will suffice." I
am brought to the classroom. There are about 15 students sitting in a semicircle behind
tables and Ahuva and another teacher stand at the back to observe. Before opening
my folder, I open my pelvis, *mula bandha*, and feel a calmness enter my breathing. I
have handouts; we talk about the meanings of the words *innocence* and *experience*. It is
surprising that innocence is not a thing unto itself but rather a lack of experience, the
state of not yet knowing. We look at "Nurse's Song" in *Innocence*; a student raises her
hand, asks why the meter changes in the last lines.

'Well, well, go and play till the light fades away,
And then go home to bed.'
The little ones leaped and shouted and laughed
And all the hills echoed.

In a flash, I recall Allen's voice from an earlier time; I hear him address this very issue!

"Well you see, the children are circling the nurse and pleading 'please, please.' After the nurse gives permission to 'go and play', the children jump up and run off and so does the meter." The student blurts out, "Good answer!" As I teach, I notice that Ahuva looks interested but the other teacher has a terrifying scowl on her face. I feel there is no chance of being hired!

After the lesson, I meet another English teacher, Audrey, who talks to me as if I already have the job. I am confused and don't take these hints seriously. The following week, I'm surprised to hear that the school is interested in hiring me. I must come in for the head of school interview. Roanna asks me if there is anything she needs to worry about if she searches for me online. I'm ready for this. In my self-search, I find two items of concern on the first page of results. One is a poem called "Loving Monogamy," which pornographically extols my marriage in fabliau style. I write it to confound the likes of the sanctimonious Senator Jesse Helms; I dedicate it to the Senator. The poem is on Al Aronowitz's *Blacklisted Writers* website. I know his son, the photographer Myles Aronowitz; he scrubs the poem out for me. But harder to expunge is an essay I write for a collection of essays on LSD. The essay is not published in the print volume but is posted on the website. I ask the editor to take it down, which he does; however, an empty link to the article called "Psychedelic Adventures" remains on Google.

I tell Roanna that she would see a link to an expunged article about the use of psychedelics. She is concerned and credits me for being forthright. I assure her that these psychedelic investigations are in the past. She asks me what I would say about drug use if a student asks me. I tell her that I would suggest activities like drama club; acting provides an out-of-body sense of belonging and purpose. I also promise to try again to get that link erased. Roanna tells me that she will think this over and get back to me. I call the editor of the psychedelic collection and ask what it takes to remove the link. This is out of his control. It is a server issue. I tell him that this is very important to me. Like many other people in the early new millennium, I am beginning to understand the indelibility of an online trail. He bugs the people at the server who do indeed eliminate the empty link. I get the job, but a wary eye is upon me.

I tell Brian, my department head at City Tech, where I adjunct, that I will not be coming back. He tells me that he would take me back if I want to come back later. When I start at City Tech eight years back, I ask Brian what's the biggest mistake I can make. "Make paperwork for me!" This seemingly innocuous remark has a deep resonance for me. I realize I must handle all problems within my classroom; no student ever goes to the department head to complain about me or, worse yet, make charges against me. If an occasional student misses one of the two required final exams and has a good record with assignments, I can extrapolate the missing exam score. The job is measured in the clean and completed class folder turned in at the end of the term. I spend unpaid hours working with challenged students to help them outside the class. My best class observation score is a time that I am ten minutes late to class because of a train breakdown. The class waits for me; the observer is impressed. It shows how reliable

I am that the students have such confidence in my arrival. Teaching four college classes a week is much easier than teaching four classes a day in high school. Grade-school teaching is grounded in the trenches of education.

The routine of grade-school teaching is nonstop. Adding up: 8:00 a.m. to 5:00 p.m. dual curriculum, two to three hours of lesson planning or grading essays each night. Each night finds me blurry-eyed at its end. I need to sleep and will not if I think about school; I train myself to not recall classroom experiences on late-night risings, fearing a failure to regain sleep. I rise at 5:45 a.m. to spend a sacred half-hour with coffee at my kitchen window. My shirts are arranged blues to the left of greens, each with a preselected tie on its shoulder; I dress in total darkness as Rochelle breaths the deep oblivion of sleep. Tenth Street is still mostly dark when I leave home. For the first time in my life I really love erev Shabbat. My teaching grind comes to a stop on Shabbat. The school is half day, the time before Shabbat is free, and the Shabbat itself remains wholly unspent. Sunday is mostly given over to my homework; I am lucky to get three essays graded in an hour. Teaching at Heschel High makes me love the seasons, especially the season of baseball. The work becomes a ten-year tunnel with temporary lights strung along as rhythmical years.

Who is gawking more? The students see another overweight Jewish man with a beard. I see young women and young men 15, 16, 17 years old. They understand something I have yet to learn. They have all the power. I remember being in high school where all power is deferred. I hide in plain view. In a way, I am shocked by how much it is the same and how much it is different here. Most new to me is the gender-neutral atmosphere. I, being perceived as straight male, provide lawful flirting possibilities for some and (being not completely straight) offer alternate role-modeling to others. I soon learn that the administrators gossip with the students; students informally determine the teachers' progress reports.

I am slowly brought on board. I only have three classes in my first year as well as other duties, which include yearbook advisor, and college essays coach. I am barely observed, and although I probably do little harm, my teaching chops are not yet firing on all cylinders.

Before starting at Heschel High, I make it to a 7:00 A.M. morning *minyan* every weekday at Town & Village Synagogue. I tell Ahuva that the minyan needs me in their number and will *kill me* if I drop out. She allows me to come in a little late to attend my minyan. But Heschel offers four morning minyanim every day. Teachers aren't required to attend, but all students are. Second year, I switch to Heschel's egalitarian minyan, led by Rabbi Dahlia who is a little person. I find her spiritual commitment hugely compelling. She becomes my uptown rabbi. I become more deeply embedded in the fabric of the school. It becomes family. I enjoy the Shabbatonim in the woods. *Davening* with students helps me join the students in true friendship. Dahlia knows I am a writer. She hands me a well-known homiletic blessing for one's house that is sometimes framed on a family's kitchen wall. She asks me to reinterpret it to extend the blessing to the all-school Shabbaton. I joyfully do so. She is shocked at the liberties I take, but when I read it to the whole school, she gets it.

HOUSE BLESSING

May our fleeting walls hold lasting joy and peace
We are bricks
Shabbat is the mortar of our strength
As we contemplate our stillness
Friendships are made solid
Our hands join to raise the roof to our future
Like rocks that sing in the waves
Our voices lap Holy Words against our lips
All thought is holy when we gather
Underneath God's being

The students are likable, wide open with approvals and dislikes; they don't yet know how to create true insight for themselves. A well-placed true observation makes a big difference. Every so often, one watches a student light up with sudden comprehension; take a leap in the ability to analyze text with insight. These occasions, although rare, are enough to let teachers know that they are treading in the right direction.

In my second year, one of my tenth-grade students is the daughter of a powerful New York City family. The daughter adopts me. She offers to help me. I must seem fumbling, unsure of myself. She understands her inherent power and my inherent weakness. Her mother is aware of something. At the parent-teacher conferences, none of my colleagues warn me to be on my toes for this parent. Instead of me handling the conversation, the mother turns it into a job interview. She questions the value of my assignments and demands glib rationales. I have been teaching rhetorical forms of essay writing. Learning to control one's language develops mental rigor. I don't express my ideas smoothly. I puzzle her just enough to make the minutes go by; the encounter remains a standoff. Afterward, teachers surround me to find out how it went. They explain that this woman grills everybody. "Why didn't you tell me?" "Would it have helped?" Ah, the time-honored theory of sink or swim!

The mother does tell Ahuva to fire me. Ahuva protects me because she understands that the recipe for becoming a fully competent teacher is five years in the classroom. One can learn how to lesson plan, how to assess progress, engage discussion, manage behavior, but no one can teach how to teach. The essence of teaching is to create an open space. The student is invited to enter this new space and learn the use of new tools. Students secretly soak in the love that the teacher secretly expresses; they must sense safety while performing new mental acrobatics.

Adolescents are endowed with a dramatic sense of finality about grades. My particular skill is converting perceived failure into a road map for learning. A C-plus grade on a tenth-grade paper elicits tears; they moan that they will never get into college! I assure students that no matter how they do in tenth grade; they are all going to college. "This is the time to make mistakes and to learn from them. Colleges want to see improvement in your grades; this shows that you are capable of learning." My favorite grade is B-plus because it indicates a sure comprehension of both the topic and the task. The *very good* grade indicates excellent ideas, maybe even experimental ideas, but there might be an organizational issue or grammatical fault. The A student might grow complacent and lose the ability to reach further than their grasp, in case they fall a little. The B-plus student achieves more. Do students buy this argument? No way! They grouse about receiving my *favorite grade* on their essays.

My second year becomes horrible. I am being observed more. I am getting a lot of negative critical feedback from Ahuva and Audrey. I am not yet fully clicking with the tenth graders. I need to make myself equally accessible to all in the class. I need to grade papers more thoroughly. I wake up each day with dread of getting out of bed. I trudge to school sick with fear in my stomach. One of my big issues is that I have dysgraphia, which disables my ability to see words in my head. I can't spell as most people do. If asked to spell out a word, most people see the word and read off the letters. I don't see the word. I have to learn to spell each word through phonetic tricks. I am the English teacher that cannot spell. Writing on the chalkboard terrifies me. The year is half over; my misery is unabated.

I request a meeting with Audrey, my department head, and Sandra, my veteran mentor. It is Sandra's frown that I notice at my model lesson. I soon discover her fierce loyalty and wicked humor. I tell them that I plan to quit in June. They look shocked. They tell me not to make any decision yet. Audrey says to give it another year for their sake; they promise to give me more help. Sandra says that I am really close to becoming an excellent teacher; I should hang in there. I agree to try again. I am happy because I finally hear some positives about my teaching rather than my deficiencies.

My first year, I have facing desks with a veteran teacher who transferred from another school. He is working a single year at Heschel as a transition to retirement. In some ways, we are both first-year teachers; he shares lesson planning skills with me, I interpret the Jewish world for him. I see the abundantly marked-up graded papers he returns to students. When he is actually retired, I call him and hire him to teach me how to annotate essays. He is thorough and simple; I realize it is not more difficult than what I am already doing. He has a system to organize the critical feedback: underscore in text, comment in margin, reiterate and expand the comments with advice in a summation at the bottom of the end-page. Soon my comments become more effective. I make comments in the margins that illustrate the broken rules in the highlights. This gives me more information to restate and digest to expand in closing. Furthermore, I switch my grading from hand grading to computer grading. I blow the student text up to 200 percent and take off my glasses. I walk into the essay in a way that defeats my dysgraphia. I devise a system of color-coded highlights: an awkward phrase one color, incomplete or run-on sentence another, a vague assertion another. A challenged essay looks like a rainbow. Students hate to see an essay come back full of red pencil; they can't bear to look into its glare. I am giving back ample corrective evidence to the student without shaming.

One-third of the students are diagnosed with learning issues; attention deficit disorder is most common. They are medicated, and the nurse's office is a crowded dispensary at lunch. Diagnosed students are allowed extra time on in-class assessments. A diagnosis by a psychologist must be respected. This diagnosis can be purchased from some psychologists. The English department is tough. We require all essays to be written in-class. If they write essays at home, it invariably becomes the work of tutors and parents. When they have extra-time, I have to collect their work at the end of the period until the start of a later period for writing. It makes grading complicated with so many students completing their work at different times. I feel comfortable occasionally extending time for an undiagnosed student who needs it. We assign an essay every two weeks, so there is a lot of essay grading.

I switch to using Google docs for essay assignments. This allows me to easily share and unshare the document with each student. Now I control the extra time, use color grade marks on the document, furthermore I am able to check the student's writing for cheating, such as, large insertions. The class becomes almost paperless. Audrey is now satisfied with the amount and quality of my feedback.

Sandra is the dean of the eleventh grade and a venerable leader of the English department. She coaches debate. Sandra brooks fools poorly. She has perfected the enigmatic frowning-teacher face. Her actions belie her frown. She is incredibly helpful to those smart enough to ask. I enjoy discussing the literature with her. She has strong literary arguments but in every way wants to hear mine. We can talk about the merits of each argument. She gives me a wrapped present; I find the gift on my desk. Read the card and exclaim, "Oh shock! Horror!" Sandra is utterly delighted with my response. I know we are like siblings. I help her on field trips and on away debates. She helps me to turn my poetic parent reports into understandable pedagogy.

I have difficulty following a mechanical lesson plan because I am a creative teacher. An adherence to a plan becomes wooden and lifeless. My own plans propose guideposts and criteria for class discussion. I allow sudden new routes to pop up.

Expository writing is very difficult for the many students that are not reading closely. Students mostly don't engage with the text or ask questions of the text. Reading is a physical activity. It physically affects each of us as we read. I notice that I sometimes get a queasy stomach at points in a story while reading. I mark that passage and later go back to see why I reacted. Once there, I always discover a basis for analysis: narrative shift, repeated reference, character change. I apply elements of literary analysis based on my digestion. I teach students to read themselves as they read text to discover their own physical tells. Original thinking is easy when one is reading dynamically.

At a regional school conference on teaching, I mention this concept of reading oneself while one reads to a table of high-school language and literature teachers and a college professor, the keynote speaker. A teacher across the table immediately pushes back as if I am off my rocker. The professor interrupts him and says that I am spot-on, that he wishes more high-school teachers would teach this way. Later the head of the conference makes an effort to say goodbye to me.

Creativity is disappearing in both teachers and students. Teachers teach what they learn in graduate education courses, and students write to the expectations of programmed teaching plans to get high grades. The results now are college graduates who can't problem-solve or commit themselves to original thinking. Read yourself as you read.

I expand my sense of analytical space into structuring the five-paragraph essay; create a method for essay construction rather than a formula. The opening paragraph contains a good thesis that creates space for an answer with intellectual merit. The three body paragraphs populate the written space with analytical precision. I insist there be three distinct diagnostic divisions to support the thesis; with each division utilizing an identifiable analytical argument, for example, a narrator observation, the use of symbolism, a setting argument. Each argument supports the thesis in a different way and is, in turn, itself supported by textual evidence.

Most students are writing book report summations of plot and character. I force them to expand their skills by adding an argument that cites the structure of the writing. I make the students fully sentence outline the essay: a thesis statement, three body paragraph topic sentences, the relevant text proofs. The essay is essentially written; the students learn how to frame their own insights effectively in a composition of original thought. After a few years, I am teaching and reading, writing, giving solid feedback, and getting results. My fears are gone. I know what I embody as a teacher. Students trust me enough to learn. Now parents want me as their child's teacher.

*

In the eleventh grade we read Arthur Miller's *Death of a Salesman*. Like much drama, it tracks power shifts between principal characters. The brothers, Biff and Happy, are the nucleus of the play. Their father, Willy Loman, is metaphorically dead before the play opens. The boys' cruelty toward Willy is more painful to endure than Willy's life of cruelty to all around him. Willy is stuck orbiting the mass of the broken-down American dream. His sons' callousness is deliberate, whereas his is helplessly being pulled under by waves of a changing society. The Loman obsession with success prevents them from finding it.

We examine the staging and the arc of each character. Willy becomes a part of the setting as he walks through the stage walls and the walls of time. Willy's tragic character flaws kill him. His narcissistic anger scares us so much that we focus on the two sons.

Happy seems successful and independent. Biff is lost, unable to manage his own life. These boys contrast the post world war economic boom's seemingly easy path to success. The world is sagging under the weight of human failure.

The cost of global distress is apparent in the students' lives: degradation to the environment, stratification of the social classes and genders, shrinking of job security, measurement of success in *likes* and not productivity. Adult children today need their parents love the way Biff needs Willy's approval. Willy cannot give that approval because he is frozen in his inability to accept his own failures; the play is suspended in time.

*

The boys rarely ask to meet with me. They get disappointed, then they act sullen. I notice that most girls seek me out for help and support. Cultural forces that no one fully fathoms are sweeping all of them along. The boys rarely strategize ways to improve themselves; instead they blame others, especially women, for raising the bar to success. Boys still labor under the patriarchal delusion that women exist to enhance men. It is maddening to men that women find identity in other women rather than being appended to a male. Valuing women less than men floats false male equivalency. I can only hope men learn to become self-reliant buoys bobbing beside self-reliant women.

When a young man is unable to participate in class discussion, I give him what I call my "Invitation to the Table" talk. I am offering a feast. Young men do not feel invited to the table. They feel that they are being blamed for the patriarchal sins of the their forbearers. If they are deemed guilty without having adequate time to mature, then why try to be pleasant? "Pull up a chair and I will serve you. Raise your hand and I will call on you. I will even rehearse with you to formulate a question and answer just to get you started." It often works.

Some female teachers do ignore under-functioning males. The young men feel disliked; they are branded as distasteful. Their quirkiness is deemed laziness. They can't color between the lines. These young men are me. I invite them to improve their writing by showing them how to organize their thoughts. I call on them and validate their ideas in discussion. They shape up nicely. Moms notice. I am being asked for because I know what it is like to be passed over in school.

All the students are pressured to perform well and get good grades. One of my male advisees tells me he wants to be a chef. I encourage him to apply to culinary schools. His parents are not happy. I assure them that there is nothing easy about culinary school; it involves a lot of math and chemistry. In the end, the parents realize that their son is now focused on something he likes; gets better grades overall. He does go to a culinary school.

My class discussions evolve away from what Sandra calls "spit back." We, the class and me, create questions that become critical thinking; we establish an arena of success. I let my eagerness to learn from the students thrill them into original contributions. When I don't glance up at the clock until the last minute of class, the discussion is a success.

Because I have a learning disability, I am able to straight-talk kids diagnosed with learning disabilities. My undiagnosed dysgraphia makes my grade-school hard. My mother drills me with endless spelling books. Nothing helps; I am dumb. Because I become a writer despite the inability to spell, I understand how these students struggle.

When I first write poetry, I hear a pounding beat in my head as I bang out the lines on a manual typewriter. The words appear on paper as if by magic because I do not see them until they are embossed there. I dialogue with the entity that writes poetry with me. My dysgraphia mixes with synesthesia to create a driving aural meter. I tell students who struggle with a disability that they must believe that the disability is a reward rather than a curse. It is a gift that gives back after one works hard to succeed with it. "When you learn to write on a nuts-and-bolts level, you will become a better writer than the naturally talented student who has no idea how it works!" I warn them it is hard, and they cry; but they know that I am right. They have no other hope or choice.

*

Biff and Happy watch their father closely. Their imaginary love for their mother, Linda, becomes a form of cruelty as they callously try to protect her from Willy's delusions. But Willy is not suffering true delusions. They transform him into pure allegory, the bankrupt dream of commerce. Both sons abandon their father in a restaurant bathroom. Biff resents Willy's false promise. Now that Willy is utterly vulnerable, Biff gives him a proverbial kick. The redemption of Willy's tragic demise is that Biff might find himself. Every parent grows old; becomes a dot matrix of weaknesses. Every child hates to realize they too will waste away. Willy's ultimate delusion is that he can save the family by killing himself. Yes, the insurance does pay off the house. But as Willy states in act one, scene one, and Linda echoes it the coda: "Figure it out. Work a lifetime to pay off a house. You finally own it, and there's nobody to live in it." Voluntary suicide is never heroic. The real tragedy is that Willy is no more gone than he is present at the curtain.

Happily, I tell myself, "I am not Willy." Teaching teenagers is an act of pure fatherhood. I listen well and offer comfort. I invite the student to a feast of possibilities and new ways to digest the richness of the diet. As students light up with ideas, I feel valuable. I always want the beating heart of existence between us. Yet like Willy, I wash away with time's persistence. For me, students become the lasting truth that embodies light arising from an empty stage.

*

The value of teaching is found in the ability to correct one's own faults. Besides inviting young men to the table of intellectual expansion, I counsel them one on one. I want them to open up to analytic ideas and emotive concepts in their writing. Often it's a matter of generosity – not to protect oneself so tightly that no human connectivity slips through. Their fathers still counsel them to keep their feelings under control. It is not mannish to uncover them. I let boys know there is a way to maintain a tough bearing and share intimate knowledge with non-embarrassing tactics. Men are committed to a hierarchical logic that if they twist ideas far enough, an inner core of emotional truth can shine through. I can only inspire them through example. I share my weakness in a strong manner. Now I tell classes that I can't spell. No longer afraid to write on the board, I hold the erasable marker on the white board, and call out to the class, "Is it *e a* or *a e?*" A student, paying attention, tells me without derision. Students do not complain to their parents about my lack of spelling prowess. There is enough I do tell them including how to know what they don't know; that is what sticks. One mother tells me, "You are quiet, but you have a lot to say."

I am occasionally asked to substitute as a leader in the men's minyan. I hope to raise discussions on challenges facing men. But there is no interest. It is too early in the morning. It is easier to stay embedded in a delusion of anger. Tough love breaks down personal resistance; it can be an effective tool to force young men to gain empathy. But I also believe that men can be honored and brought out of their fears in a less severe atmosphere. The benefit of doing the *work* of transforming has to be spelled out clearly.

A young man wants to leave my class and go into a class for challenged learners because he figures that he will get higher grades. He is struggling with Hawthorne's *The Scarlet Letter*. His father owns a successful retail business. I tell him that if he can master Hawthorne's deeply perceptive psychological acuity, then someday he will be able to analyze salespeople that walk into his office before they sit down. He gets the point. He learns to frame his reactions to literature in a well-organized essay. The direct appeal to practical applications helps him overcome the fear of failing.

I am a flawed teacher; teaching institutions keep employees' job security uncertain. I am on probation for eight of my ten years at the school. My faults are minor compared with my abilities. My worst moment comes at my twelfth grade drama class's theater trip to the Irish Rep Theater. Uniform British soldiers stand guard up the aisles before the curtain of an Irish play about the troubles. This is a great theatrical device, easy to notice. Rochelle meets us at the theater, tells me my Mother's health has just taken a serious downturn. I am listening to her report; paying scant attention to my one obnoxious student harassing one of the soldiers. She is trying to get him to break character. The play starts before I can stop her. The actor involved writes a handwritten complaint to the head of school: two more years' probation for me. It is not a monetary punishment and in no way curtails rights and privileges. Ahuva has to keep me on probation; she asks me to write to her about my teaching. I write about my writing program, my method of feedback, critical analysis practices, and approach to reading literature. In a long letter to me, Ahuva uses all these good qualities and pedagogical accomplishments to praise me as a teacher and then, in the last paragraph, informs me that I am punished.

At the start of my tenth year at Heschel High, I tell the assistant head of school that I will be retiring in June. She says, "We certainly don't want to see you go. You are an asset to the school." This is the highest compliment on my teaching. It means that I pay for myself in dollars and sense. Of course, workers are rarely told something like this. It might swell their heads. Parents are requesting me for sons who seem disinterested and for daughters struggling to manage a learning obstacle. My head is already swollen with literature.

I often wish I could teach *Moby Dick*. I know it is impossible to fit into the normal curriculum because: weight, heightened narrative, hyper-objective exposition, and singular universality. I finally find an opportunity to fit the novel into a four-week mini-class elective for seniors. If I slave-drive the students through the reading, they will all hate the book and gain nothing. I would be the net loser, and so would Melville. One month is not long enough to both research the novel and write a valid critical essay. The grade element will have to be how well the student reads the novel. Instead of inserting several tests, I purchase small blank books with *Moby Dick* covers and keep them in the classroom. The daily chapters to be covered are on the syllabus. I compose short prompts based on the night's pages: two straightforward short questions and one reflective long question. The students write for ten minutes in their blank books at the start of each class. I know if they are actually doing the reading. I am surprised that twenty students sign up for the course, which plainly announces it has a heavy reading requirement. Of the twenty students, four or five manage to keep up and read the whole book. Even if they only speed-read, my enthusiasm and their trust in me makes the class a joy. The door is open now. Some of them will read the novel again at leisure and get the world out of it. So much of teaching is for later; the aha moments keep coming.

*

Men are not from Mars. They don't all think in tiered absolutes. Staying on top is not a goal. Pumping iron is not a form of leadership. A redefinition of strength is. Not caving in to anger needs strength beyond muscle. Anger dissolves under direct observation. Superman is special because of his X-ray vision. Men can strip away the bullshit that hurts women and children. Men need to use their X-ray vision to see the truth inside form. Masculinity is so much better when rescued from the stale logic of domination. Real getting is discovered at the open door of giving.

*

Each classroom is a micro universe in which the student is an instrument of both participation and distraction. When this inner conflict achieves balance, learning does happen. The class dynamic is particular to the makeup of each class. If students thwart each other, the class is hard to lead. They are often afraid to share; they also fear being thought of as too engaged or too eager. When a class works well, the students are engrossed and open to fielding new ideas with one another. The teacher has to model inhabiting this open space by showing that all accurate reactions to literature can be supported by the text. Teachers are not all-knowing but rather possess the keys to finding plausible answers. As Sandra likes to answer students when they inquire if her test questions are the same each year, "The questions are the same, but the answers change." Every class is its own world. Occasionally, this world feels as if it is being born. A teacher must enjoy these moments.

At CUNY, City Tech, one class gives me a card at the end of the semester. On it, the students write wonderful messages to me; they tell me that I am the best teacher they've ever had! I am feeling so good that I show it to Brian, my department head. Big mistake. He could care less. The things he appreciates are: my students don't complain to him; I get to class on time; I fill out my class chart completely. There is nothing I can do to change my position as an adjunct teacher. Don't waste Brian's time. At Heschel, when students honor me in a special way, I keep it to myself.

The future chef in tenth grade, makes a mead-house out of gingerbread to celebrate our reading of *Beowulf*. I mention this to Sandra, who says I have to show the house to Ahuva. I trepidatiously knock on her door. Ahuva is excited and pleased.

My approach to working at Heschel is to inhabit the Heschel family. I have to be forced to be the yearbook adviser; I choose to be the advisor to the first Gay Straight Alliance Club on campus. Through Allen Ginsberg, I met David Carter, an expert on the Stonewall Uprising. On a Friday after school, he meets the club and me in front of the Stonewall Inn and describes the pitched battle, pointing out the routes for the police and the strongholds for the drag queens. I start a poetry-writing club. The students love the movie *Dead Poets Society*. We call ourselves the Living Poets Society.

I am asked to speak at a high-school assembly on the eleventh anniversary of the 9/11 disaster. I write a poem that narrates my experience of that day teaching at City Tech and laments my good friend Steven's demise atop World Trade Center's North Tower. He is the mentor that taught me how to wrap tefillin, and how to lift the Torah at chagbah. The school is in assembly in the gym and the student body is seated on the floor. It's solemn without the usual low whispering among the students. Ahuva introduces me by saying the poem shows how outside events deeply shape our lives in surprising ways. It is one of the most intense reading experiences of my life:

Eleven-Year Look Back to 9/11

In memoriam Steven Jacobson

the night before
a storm hit ahead of midnight
lightning crashed over downtown Manhattan
thunder shook the windows and several tenements were struck
frying modems and phones
the city at dawn glistened like a body emerging from the shower
streets were washed clean and the cars and street signs revealed
their true shapes without the accumulated grime
jauntily I strode down First Avenue to the F train
in a few minutes I was in downtown Brooklyn
ready to teach composition 101 in a windowless classroom at 8:30 a.m.
we were studying the first chapter of Maya Angelou's
I Know Why the Caged Bird Sings
she is a young black girl in the employ of an insensitive white woman
the woman can't pronounce the child's name and so simplifies it
in revenge, the little girl
drops a casserole dish that had been in the woman's family for generations
Angelou thoroughly describes the crashing of the dish
the confusion that ensues
at the moment of studying the words that signify
crash bang and fracture
I heard students running in the hallway
the class had ten minutes left
I paid no heed to the hallway noise
after dismissing the class
I went to the hallway to see what was up
students were gathered at the windows that faced the Battery
there they were
two blazing towers
trick candles that cannot be blown out
the students and I stood watching for several minutes
the first tower lurched a bit
a gasp
then the first tower slowly collapsed into itself
I thought
here I am on the plains of the Holy Land
watching the Tower of Babel as it falls
there was some laughter among the students

the nervous laughter that signifies
an inability to respond
I spoke for the first time
"A lot of people just died"
a Muslim student lifted his hands in an open gesture
and praised God in Arabic
at that moment the loudspeakers crackled to evacuate the building
I had no cell phone then
besides, the cell phone towers weren't working
I had a tiny radio and turned on the all-news AM
the sidewalks were jammed
people were randomly going nowhere fast
the radio said that there were five more planes in the air waiting to strike
the police had no orders
I walked to the Manhattan Bridge
to be stopped and ordered away
there was no going into Manhattan
I sat in a small triangle of grass at the Brooklyn
foot of the Manhattan Bridge
watched the continual stream of shocked people coming out of Manhattan
women in high heels gratefully flung off their shoes
dropped onto the grass
people talked to themselves and those around them
"I was in the subway going to work and an intense air pressure hit us
made the tunnel shake
I was evacuated and ran out of there"
I sat for hours thinking about high-speed trains
we need high-speed trains in this country
they cannot be driven into buildings
there was no way to call my wife or mother in California
mid-afternoon a lady came by, told all of us that they had opened
a halfway house down the street
bathrooms and telephone
I waited in line and finally called my wife
we then knew we were both alive
I had no idea when travel back to Manhattan would resume
late afternoon I heard that the F train was running
I went into Manhattan in a jammed subway car
when I popped up at First Avenue and Houston
there were lost-looking soldiers giving directions
no one was allowed below Houston

I made my way home
the bars were full
everyone seemed drunk on fear or booze
as soon as I got into my own home
I remembered Steve
Steve is a stalwart member of our morning minyan at Town & Village Synagogue
Steve worked all night as an engineer for WPIX (channel 11)
he worked at the top of the World Trade Center
underneath the big broadcast antennae
he opened the chapel every morning before 7:00 a.m. when he got off work
Steve had taught me so much
he taught me how to wrap tefillin my first time
I copied his *minhag* since I had none of my own
I remembered that Steve had been happy that his schedule
finally had been switched from all night to all day
I prayed that he had made minyan
I called a fellow minyanaire
asked, "Did Steve open the shul today?"
a sad, sad no was the reply
I sat in my living room
my face in my hands
wept
to this day I have a hard time
looking at hagbah lest one of the Twin Towers of Torah
falls before my eyes

Afterward, several students tell me they want to be poets. The head of the school, who had been so unhappy with me over the actor's complaint, calls the program riveting.

*

The school receives a Jewish Educational grant to integrate Judaic and secular studies. Dov, a religious studies teacher, and I create a special senior seminar. It combines Judaic philosophy and world literature. I ask the students to read Dostoyevsky's *The Idiot* over the summer. I caution them to make the fat book their friend; take it everywhere – to camp, to the beach, to Israel. It is a gamble to assign a long novel, but it pays off. The students fall in love with the book. We enjoy it in depth and use Myshkin's character as a touchstone all year. One combination of texts that works extremely well is Soloveitchik's *The Lonely Man of Faith* and Camus's *The Stranger*. Dov and I are both patient teachers and coordinate well. Dov opens up spiritual overtones and contextual urgencies in the Jewish text; I lead detailed explorations of the literary texts, which reveal that the words become animate by mixing them with the spiritual texts. We teach the same course again the following year but this time the students sign up for the wrong reasons. They intend to take advantage of our laidback natures. They hate and don't read the Dostoyevsky, and they refuse to discuss any of the texts. A deadly feeling overcomes the class. Dov starts to lecture at length to make the minutes go by while no one listens. I drift in and out a little; a student reports me for sleeping in class. Once again I am destined to be on the outs with the bosses. Ahuva is nice about it but is obliged to keep me on probation and suggests I get checked out for sleep apnea. I do not blame Dov's loquaciousness. We don't continue the grant the following year. It is utterly amazing one year and a total waste the second. It is impossible to deliberately design the perfect class for the perfect students. But it does happen; I bet I am not alone remembering.

I near my retirement. When hired, I tell Ahuva I hope to teach ten years. I will be 66 years old at the end of the 2015 – 2016 school year. Social Security starts for me at the end of that summer. My last year is like my first. I am left alone. We have a new head of school, a new head of high school, and a new department head. Books we used to teach in the tenth grade, such as *Brave New World,* are no longer taught. The students are able to read it; the new teachers are not willing to teach it. Parents and students lobby the school to allow academic essays to be written at home instead of in one fifty-minute class. Tutors and parents can now facilitate the writing. I am glad to bow out; the old-school writing is on my wall.

I use most of my summers to write *Straight Around Allen: On the Business of Being Allen Ginsberg.* I need more than just a few summer weeks to finish it. Teaching high school provides me my best salary. I put away as much as I am allowed into retirement funds. The ten years work doubles what my monthly social security benefit would have been if I had remained off the books. I avoided professional career-like jobs until I was 55 years old; ten years on the grade-school chain gang! After working in the Allen Ginsberg world for thirty years I needed to prove to myself that I can succeed in life without the bard's attachment. Success is a feeling of accomplishment best understood by one's self.

Working is always the means to a beginning. I am no longer a laborer, a messenger, a housecleaner, a bookkeeper, or a secretary. I remain a teacher and an artist. In an event of pure serendipity The New York Review of Books offers to reprint *Cleaning Up New York* in their Little Book Room series of quirky editions about New York City. Henry Wessels, a book dealer, whose wife, Mary Jo, had worked in the Ginsberg office, loves my old publication and gives it to select people as a lost treasure. He is helping the New York Review of Books catalog their archives; and they are one of the recipients. I fall on the floor laughing. I am overjoyed to be both almost retired and a "genuine" writer!

There are several teachers I will miss, but Sandra, my mentor, sister, desk mate, will be greatly missed. As spring nears, I start to carry home the books I have assembled. I am honored in my minyan; Dahlia weaves moments for me to recite my poems during the morning service. I read poems that I had written for it or had read there before.

Sandra gathers these writings and makes a small edition of a dozen copies. I am much fussed over. The whole student body heartily cheers me at the farewell assembly. They shake my hand; I know that we have all succeeded together. I feel the original joy of teaching and sharing. The year before, Ahuva decides to leave, she calls her favorite teachers into her office individually to offer each a single word that represents her appreciation. My word is *gravitas*.

*

In the *Death of a Salesman*'s coda there is a reordering of the world. Charlie, Willie's neighbor, speaks in faux-Shakespearian clarity, "Nobody dast blame this man." Willy releases Biff from the stranglehold of despair and hypocrisy; Biff is awoken and Happy is slow to grasp this change. Willy's final and only success is found in those around him. Linda's last ironic line, "We're free," is the working person's credo. Work all your days; pay off your mortgage; there is Death lounging in the doorway. Welcome home. The young men will make their peace with their fathers. Willy is not gone in their dreams. They too become fathers and teach the lessons of fatherhood as they are.

Soon Born Future

For Ace Rosenthal

the hard part about children having children
we are all broken vessels that once were whole
a child soaks up more than a parent can prevent
and being the keener of the two
is the glue that words can't break
even if the world cracks up
an easy salve to apply is full attention to the child
when first impregnated with the future memories
open doors long shut tight with gentle anguish
air the vacant child's room – rattle open windows
sweep the corners out – add a future of bright colors
and steady embraces to hold the world together
it all makes sense when a baby fits your palm

I want to open the doors long battered and scuffed
to grasp a child again and breath in a concert of generations
sing a lullaby whose softness accepts the entirety
of being alive under a night sky
where my love is always found
for my children and my children's children
in a bright star that can guide them

Bob Rosenthal was born in Chicago, 1950. He and his partner moved to the Lower East Side to avoid careers in 1973. He worked as a Walking Messenger, an Urban House Cleaner, a Bookkeeper in a Country & Western Nightclub, High School English Teacher, Poetry Art Worker, and Secretary to Poet Allen Ginsberg.

Fifth Avenue Overhead is his 3rd volume of Bob's personal prose, which includes *Straight Around Allen: On the Business of Being Allen Ginsberg*/Beatdom Books 2019 and *Cleaning Up New York*/Angel Hair 1977: republished by The Little Bookroom 2016.

Bob's poetry books are: *Morning Poems*/Yellow Press, *Lies About the Flesh*/Frontward Books, *Rude Awakenings*/Yellow Press, and *Viburnum*/White Fields Press.

Bob's plays with Bob Holman are: *The Cause of Gravity*, *The Whore of the Alpines*, *Bicentennial Suicide* and Ted Berrigan's *Clear the Range*.

He lives in New York.

ACKNOWLEDGMENTS

I am grateful to many people serving as early readers: Rochelle Kraut, Richard Friedman, Simon Schuchat, Henry Condell, Marion Ferrier, and Sandra Silverman. I owe a special debt of gratitude to Steve Levine and Rod Smith for their indispensable reading.

Book layout and design by Jo Scoville.

STRAIGHT AROUND ALLEN
On the Business of
Being Allen Ginsberg

by Bob Rosenthal

On *Straight Around Allen: On the Business of Being Allen Ginsberg*

> It's an amazingly interesting book, . . . Well written, with . . .
> wisdom presented without any hubris.
>
> —Ed Sanders

> It was riveting and unlike any memoir I've ever read in structure and tone,
> very in the moment, present, candid.
>
> —Ben Shaffer

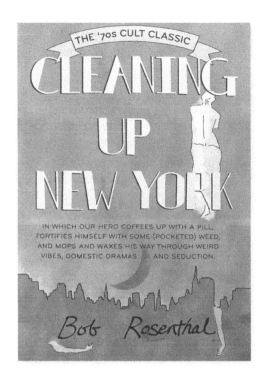

THE '70s CULT CLASSIC

CLEANING UP NEW YORK

IN WHICH OUR HERO COFFEES UP WITH A PILL,
FORTIFIES HIMSELF WITH SOME (POCKETED) WEED,
AND MOPS AND WAXES HIS WAY THROUGH WEIRD
VIBES, DOMESTIC DRAMAS ... AND SEDUCTION.

Bob Rosenthal

On *Cleaning Up New York*

It's one of those great, rare works the style of which – immaculate with
unexpected descriptor glints, and funny, low-key frankness – perfectly
embodies its subject.

—Richard Hell

There is not one wasted or misplaced word in this chronicle . . .

—Lucy Sante

EDGE BOOKS

Integrity & Dramatic Life Anselm Berrigan $10.00

Primitive State Anselm Berrigan $15.00

Some Notes on My Programming Anselm Berrigan $15.00

They Beat Me Over the Head with a Sack Anselm Berrigan $5.00

Zero Star Hotel Anselm Berrigan $18.00

Once Upon a Neoliberal Rocket Badge Jules Boykoff $14.00

The Accordion Repertoire Franklin Bruno $16.00

Cipher/Civilain Leslie Bumstead $14.00

Crow Leslie Bumstead and Rod Smith, Eds. $10.00

FPO Kevin Davies $20.00

Comp. Kevin Davies $15.00

The Golden Age of Paraphernalia Kevin Davies $18.00

Shell Game Jordan Davis $18.00

American Whatever Tim Davis $14.00

The Julia Set Jean Donnelly $6.00

Ladies Love Outlaws Buck Downs $5.00

Marijuana Softdrink Buck Downs $15.00

Tachycardia: Poems 2010–2012 Buck Downs $20.00

clearing without reversal Cathy Eisenhower $15.00

World Prefix Harrison Fisher $6.00

Metropolis 16–20 Rob Fitterman $5.00

Metropolis XXX: The Decline and Fall of the Roman Empire Rob Fitterman $14.00

One Hundred Etudes Benjamin Friedlander $18.00

Dick Cheney's Heart Heather Fuller $18.00

Dovecote Heather Fuller $14.00

perhaps this is a rescue fantasy Heather Fuller $14.00

Defender Drew Gardner $16.00

Flarf Orchestra (audio CD) Drew Gardner $12.00

Flarf: An Anthology of Flarf Drew Gardner, Nada Gordon, Sharon Mesmer, K. Silem Mohammad, and Gary Sullivan, Eds. $33.00

Terminal Humming K. Lorraine Graham $16.00

Non/Fiction Dan Gutstein $16.00

Sight Lyn Hejinian and Leslie Scalapino $15.00

Late July Gretchen Johnsen $4.00

Mannerism Deirdre Kovac $18.00

In the Works Doug Lang $20.00

Breathalyzer K. Silem Mohammad $15.00

The Sense Record and Other Poems Jennifer Moxley $14.00

Heteronomy Chris Nealon $20.00

Plummet Chris Nealon $15.00

Catalytic Exteriorization Phenomenon Mel Nichols $17.50

Stepping Razor A.L. Nielsen $10.00

Ace Tom Raworth $14.00

Caller and Other Pieces Tom Raworth $12.50

Structure from Motion Tom Raworth $18.00

Dogs Phyllis Rosenzweig $5.00

Interval Kaia Sand $14.00

The Centos Simon Schuchat $12.00

Cusps Chris Stroffolino $5.00

Long Term Raisin Ryan Walker $16.00

Felonies of Illusion Mark Wallace $15.00

Haze: Essays, Poems, Prose Mark Wallace $14.00

Nothing Happened and Besides I Wasn't There Mark Wallace $9.50

This Can't Be Life Dana Ward $16.00

AERIALMAGAZINE

edited by Rod Smith

Aerial 10: Lyn Hejinian (edited with Jen Hofer) $40.00

Aerial 9: Bruce Andrews $25.00

Aerial 8: Barrett Watten $40.00

Aerial 6/7: featuring John Cage $30.00

Literature published by Aerial/Edge is available through Small Press Distribution (www.spdbooks.org; 1-800-869-7553; orders@spdbooks.org) or from the publisher at Edge Books c/o Bridge Street Books, 2814 Pennsylvania Ave NW, Washington DC 20007. When ordering from Aerial/Edge directly, add $3.50 postage for individual titles. Two or more titles postpaid. For more information, please visit our Web site at www.aerialedge.com.